Praises for *Girl, I'm Not Trippin', I'm Depressed*

Chanita is a super mom, an amazing philanthropist, and a hardworking entrepreneur. Her sincerity and vulnerability are some of her most amazing assets that allow her to empower others, even when life is not easy!

- Kandi Burruss (Entertainer | Entrepreneur) -

I would classify Chanita as one of God's guarantors, holding the marker on making each person that reads this book accountable to face their own struggles with transparency, for the purpose of healing, by sharing her testimony so openly.

- Tami Roman (Actress | Producer) -

This book has been written by a fighter, who has overcome challenges and won many battles. Through her transparency, she proclaims that the rest of your days can be the best of your days if you would just decide to never give up. Winning is the only option!

- Marvin Sapp (Minister | Gospel Recording Artist)

# Girl, I'm Not Trippin', I'm Depressed

ISBN: 978-0-9985210-2-2

Printed in the United States of America.
First Printing, 2017.

13th & Joan
500 N. Michigan Avenue, Suite #600
Chicago, IL 60611

WWW.13THANDJOAN.COM

# Dedication

This book is dedicated to all of the women around the world that have ever felt hopeless, lost, confused, hurt, lonely, and sometimes crazy! I am you and you are me! You aren't crazy. Girl, stop tripping. You are not crazy, you are depressed! Keep going, and know that all the power that you will ever need, you already have.

# Epigraph

"When you can no longer construct a future in your mind, depression has taken over. It must be stopped at all costs."

Chanita Foster

# Foreword

It's no secret that my life has been less than perfect. Throughout my journey, I have spoken about these less than perfect moments from many stages, ranging from the pulpits of churches, television screens, during interviews, and in the midst of intimate moments with special people who have crossed my path.

If asked to describe my life with a single word, my mind inevitably gravitates towards the word "journey." I hold this same thought to be true for all of us. With every passing day, we are tasked with new challenges and the unfolding of life to conquer. If we are still blessed to be in the land of the living, we are in a constant state of engagement from our journeys.

My journey began in Detroit. Motown! Hailed as The Motor City, my memories are still so fond. I can still smell the scent of the church, in which I created so many memories. It was in that same church, that I picked up my first instrument. And as much as the thought of my beloved Detroit makes me smile, my beginnings there were humble to say the least. As with every journey of life, there are good times, and there are bad times. Most people don't like to harp on the bad times because it's easier to think and talk about the better days. It's easier to remember what felt good and what brought a smile to our faces. Over the years of my life, I've learned that much of our journey is defined by how we maneuver through the bad times. The hard moments in our lives prepare us for greater. They shape us and mold us. The most challenging moments of our lives build us into monuments, prepared to withstand the storms that are certain. I know that by now, you have experienced a storm or two along your journey. We all have. Generally speaking, I believe that by a certain age, we have recognized that we have the skills to weather a storm. I thought that I did, but what about when life gets dark? What about when the storm disconnects us from the power, and we are forced to walk around and navigate the darkness?

These moments can best be described as raging waters. With storms come rain, sleet, and maybe even a little thunder, but the storms of life are those moments that can drown us or push us to the point of suffocation with a single twist. How do we find peace and prosperity in those moments?

My storm came in the form of depression. Although we throw the term around loosely, it is as real as the air we breathe. Depression is a real storm in the lives of many around the world. The one factor that saddens me the most, is that many people will never get diagnosed or receive the help that they need. So many will experience lonely days and sleepless nights that are what I would consider tormenting. Some will have breakdowns and feelings of hopelessness. The storm of depression is agonizing.

Aside from the emotional pitfalls of depression, there are also financial pitfalls. Many will lose it all. Financial loss amidst depression can come in the form of cars, homes, family members, you name it. There are too many people walking around, who don't know how to identify the storm of depression or what to do about it.

I'm sure you're wondering where I'm going with all of this, but stay with me. There was a time when I was overtaken by the raging winds of depression. I could not see the forest from the trees, and life as I had known it was at times unbearable. In the end, I made it! By the grace of God, I made it through. My test, for most of my life, has turned into my testimony. My dark times have turned into songs that have ministered to the hearts and souls of the world. Today, I'm thankful for each breakdown because it resulted in a breakthrough. The hard and invaluable lessons taught me about myself and God's timely grace.

There were so many moments of misunderstanding, so much peril. There were times that I was misunderstood by those closest to me. I loved and I sometimes lost. I can even admit that, at times, I was tripping.

Today, I can say with confidence that I get it. I understand that even then, I did not have the tools to express to those around me what I was personally battling. I thank God for the shift in the atmosphere and the shift in my mindset. Even as I see people who resemble drastic changes in their lives, I refrain from judgement. Life can be filled with disappointments, ups, and downs. We must never forget that every face is fighting a battle that we know nothing about. Instead of placing judgement, I now say to myself, "Naw, they're not tripping. They are depressed!"

Now, I ask that you open your hearts and minds, and learn from the empowering journey of my friend Chanita Foster. If you've ever been through a trial, and I would venture to say that we all have, this book is for you.

Sincerely,

A Man Who Beat Depression by God's Grace
Fred Hammond

# Acknowledgements

My God! I thank you every day for Loving and Saving a Sinner like me. Your Love for me is unconditional. I would have to write a million books to express the Love I have for you.

Team Foster! Amber (JaNae), Majabane (Jax), Della, Kai, Jordan, Jada, and Jersey (Boss Hog). I never knew I could love this hard. Everything I do in life is for you! I Love you so much. I work so hard to be the best mommy I can be. Thank You for sharing me with the World. I know it is hard at times, but your love and understanding has been a part of setting me free. You allow me to be me! Because of you, I get to walk in Purpose and serve others. Keep praying for me! Always remember that I make mistakes, and there is always room for me to grow and be better.

George! I remember the first time I said I wanted to write a book in 2006. You came home with a laptop that said, "To the #1 Bestseller." I've never met a man that has believed in me like you do. Your support is not always verbal, but I know you have my back! Good, Bad, or Indifferent you are one of the Best Things to ever happen to me in my Life! Thank You for my children, Adopted and Biological. Without you there is no them! Our love is just different.

Sabrina Peterson. I owe you my life! When I was sitting in that closet, you came and got me out! To this day, I don't know how you knew I was depressed, but you did! Out of all the people in the world, it was you that came to save me! We have never been ones to talk on the phone every day! Never hung out tough! Never took a vacation together, but you saved me! That let me know that you are truly assigned by God! Because of you, this book exists and I'm alive! Thank You Friend! Thank You for birthing my Son, Honor! He makes me happy when skies are grey! Lol

Stormy Wellington. This Thank You could be an entire book! All because I said, YES! I will never forget the day we met at Sabrina's, Glam University event. I was just coming out of the closet of depression, and it was my first public speaking event. Out of all the women that were in attendance, you walked up to me! Now let's be clear, you are a hustler, so I'm sure you spoke to that entire room, but I like to believe that it was God giving me my second angel. Sabrina got me out of the closet, but it was your job to keep me out! I have learned so much from you! How could I have so many college degrees and not know how to speak affirmations? Chile! You taught me how to speak life to myself on the days I wanted to run back in the closet! Should I mention the money?!? You have turned me into a documented Millionaire! Stormy Nicole Wellington coached me into a Million Dollars! I owe you and I will apply the Law of Honor for the Rest of my Life!

Eboni Elektra. When it came time to make this dream a reality, you were my quiet place! I wrote this book in the mountains at the cabin, just me and you! You gave me PEACE! Your spirit allowed me to dig deep and put it all on paper! We laughed and we cried! I will cherish that time because you taught me how to be FREE! You were a part of my growth in people! I bet I won't ask for a picture unless it's Beyoncé (inside joke) I Love you Friend! Thanks for Loving me unconditionally.

Dr. Naim Shaheed. Thank You! Thank You! Thank You! Through my writing process, you made sure I was good! Every time I called and said I need a quiet place, you said, "I got you!" There is nothing like a supportive friend. Thank you, more than words, for making this happen for me!

Jevon Sims. Every girl needs a Guy Best Friend like you! You are tough! You taught me that quitting is not an option! I don't always like what you say, but I respect it! Thank You for reminding me on the days that I thought I couldn't breathe, that all I had to do was take one breath at a time. Thank You friend. All I hear in my head is, "Finish the book, Chanita." Thanks for the push!

To my TLC Family! I am so proud to be a part of a company I call FAMILY! I'm not lying! TLC is my First, My Last, and my Only!

Dream Team South Africa! You guys have changed my life! You have been the confirmation that anything is possible with hard work, belief, and prayer! I'm so Blessed to be in business with you and helping you make your Dreams come true!

I don't want to get caught in the name game because you always forget someone! Please, if you don't see your name, it's not personal! It has nothing to do with my love for you or our relationship, but this list of names includes all the people that in some way IMPACTED my JOURNEY out of depression. Karen Ekuban, Kim Wheatley, Joi Evans, Tamme Moorehead,

Pam Endsley, DeAnna Hamilton, Sharlinda Parker, Cleo Oliver, Tokela Brown, Kandi Burruss, Zee Makhobotlela, Don Juan, Trevor Gumbi, Chimere Jackson, Johnyika Terry, Todd Tucker, Stephen Jackson, Samad Davis, Toni Griffin, Ravonne Robinson, Pam McCray, Karon Riley, Uncle Victor, Jarrod Wilkins, Sheri Riley, Nicci Gilbert Daniels, Kenny E. Lloyd, Billy Dent aka Dad, and Marvin Sapp. Each one of you needs to know that it was a single MOMENT, talk, or prayer that SAVED ME!!! I promise, you gave me food for my Soul and my Spirit at different moments and you didn't even realize it!!! Just ask me what the moment was, and I can tell you on that day how you helped save me!

To the people that hold me down on a day to day basis! Yes, the squad! Jakeem Smith, Tshepiso Molefe, Kia Kelliebrew, Lynn Hudson, Keneilwe Lekopa, Latosha Bonhart formally Jackson, Cleopatra Koopman, Barry the Web Guy, and Helen Parker aka My Mommy. You are my personal village! I couldn't do it without you!

Glam Squad. LaTasha Wright (Wright Look), Jodie Rowlands, Kasi Person, and Dontez Love. Thanks for always making me look beautiful, even when I'm crying inside.

Tshibangu. Only God. I have met a lot of people in my life. A LOT! You were personally assigned by God to me! You will be my Biggest Blessing or my Biggest lesson! Real talk! From the day I met you, you have been praying for me and it is priceless! No matter what the future holds, I will never ever discount the lessons of TRUTH you have taught me! What's life without Love and Happiness? My life will never be the same! LIVE everyday like it's your last! You are the person that reminded me to get on my KNEES and pray! You have the longest prayers ever! I'll just pray (inside joke)

Jessica Reedy. I wrote this entire book with "Better" playing on repeat!!! That song ministered to my soul! I sat and cried a million times to that song. It has been my theme song to get me through! THANK YOU for helping me through this journey through song.

Robert Traylor. They keep saying it will get easier and I keep waiting. I didn't know it until you were gone, but the lessons you taught me carry me through life. I still cry. Thanks for being my first best friend! An honest friend! Rest in Heaven until we meet again!

Last, but not Least. Fred Hammond! Come on One Time! All the calls, text, prayers, and tears! You are an Amazing human! You are one of my Best Friends in the whole wide world! (Am I allowed to say that, because that sounded kind of cheesy. Lol) I am so Blessed that I get to be a Fan and a Friend. Keep touching lives and saving souls. You have taught me life is not perfect, but life is better when you TRUST!

Nyanza Shaw, it's crazy how life is! I remember being on the Mission trip to Haiti and meeting you. You instantly became my accountability partner and attorney! You would send small reminders. Let's get the book done. Are you finished? Keep going! You were my editor. Thank you for being the stranger who believed and now my friend!

# Preface

Learning is the acquisition of knowledge or skills through experience, study, or by being taught. The key word here is, experience. In order to learn, you have to experience real life.

If we reconsider the reference to a child's development, this concept makes perfect sense. You can warn a child, "Don't touch the stove. It's hot!" And even though the child hears you and comprehends what you have said, it is possible that there is a sense of non-belief that is present. If the child reaches out to touch the stove, it is almost as if they are saying, "Let me just check." In that moment, when the adult witnesses the child reach out, it is most often repeated, "Don't touch the stove! It's hot, and it will burn you. It's dangerous." Hearing it louder and with passion the second time, the child who is curious will still question the forewarned outcome. So, what happens? Let me paint the scenario for you. The baby walks up to the stove, in fearlessness, and reaches out. Here's my favorite part. The baby turns to make sure that the person who provided the warning, is nowhere in sight. Then, it happens. The baby reaches out and touches the stove, upon which, the screaming and crying begin, amidst pain, agony, regret, and the presence of disbelief. Now, I ask you to consider, how many of us are that baby? On more occasions than I can count, I have been that baby! I, like most, have to learn through it! If pain, agony, crying (lots of crying), and screaming aren't involved, then I'm most likely not learning! This is sad, but true. I know that I'm not the only person that thinks and feels this way. I've heard it said on many occasions that, "A hard head makes a soft behind." In my prayers, I like to thank God for this big butt of mine because I have had a hard head most of my life. I am able to laugh through this lesson and scenario today because I have discovered the immense value in learning through life's challenges, even if they result from my disobedience.

I personally know that the saying, "You live and you learn," is true. That is one of the winning formulas for life. Do you know that life is divided into big math problems? Ha! Word problems. Most of us fail because we suck at math. Well, I suck at math. When too many things are in the equation, I get confused. Even when I write it out, look at it, study it, I still get confused. Only special people are good at math. I mean, that's what calculators are for, right? To get through it faster or cheat! Sound like life? Everybody wants a calculator in life, so that they can go through trials and tribulations faster and cheat. Trust me, you are thinking it and I'm just saying it.

When "Life Happens," you can Live through it, Learn through it, or you can Lose it! Losing it doesn't need to be explained in depth because losing it is far more common than we wish to admit. You would be completely lying to yourself, if you fail to admit that you have ever lost it! Admittedly, there are levels to losing it, but in my humble opinion, they can all be dangerous. When "Life Happens" and you lose, it is most often because you don't see a solution during the thick of it. The overwhelming feeling that life will never be the same overtakes you in this phase. In the midst of losing it, you take a hit, mentally, spiritually, emotionally, physically, and often financially. Losing it hurts. It hurts bad. Losing it can make you question your entire existence. It can make you question your religion. Now, you know it's deep when you start questioning the creator. That's a major flag on the play, when you allow your mind and heart to shift to foolish lines of questioning like: Is there a God? Is my mama my real mom, because I feel like I'm adopted? Is he cheating on me? He didn't really die, did he? I saw them put him in the ground, is he really dead? Are we really broke? There has to be money someplace, right? I don't have cancer, do I? I'm healthy, right?

Losing it gets deep too. I'm talking about the levels of losing it in which you start talking to yourself, having full blown conversations. You get to a point where you don't even care if someone is in the room with you. You keep talking to yourself, ignoring the fact that someone else is in the room and the fact that you sound like a crazy person. Key word "crazy". Don't you hate that word? I hate when people call me crazy. I'm like, "Don't speak that into my life." I will say this, I, Chanita Foster, have just a little crazy in me. I can't say that it's all my fault. God gave me Billy Dent as a father, and... well... you have to know him, but let's just say he gave me so many attributes and a little touch of crazy is one of them. So, by default I have a little crazy in me. I'm not talking enough crazy to get a certificate or anything. I can't get a government check for this touch of crazy, but it's just enough that when necessary, my behavior will let you know that I'm Billy Dent's daughter.

So, let's just really get to it. Live through it, learn through it, or lose it. Guess what? I lost it so much, that I went into a deep depression. That depression is what has brought me to the very moment of truth that empowered me to write this book. You might even be asking, "Why a book?" Well, I decided to write this book because depression is REAL! People are living with depression every day, and the sad thing is that some will never make it out. Although this book is not for a particular race, I can say with my whole heart that depression is not truly recognized as much as it should be in the African American community.

Based on data from a study published by the Center for Disease Control, depression affects between seventeen and twenty million Americans a year, but the CDC also finds that just 7.6 percent of African Americans sought treatment.[1] Now, again, I suck at math, but that's a lot of people. But wait, there's more. Mental health is often stigmatized in the African American community. Black women are among the most undertreated groups for depression in the nation. It's real out here y'all. There are serious consequences for untreated depression. Due to the negative stigmas surrounding mental health as a whole, there is an extreme lack of knowledge about depression. I have personally been looked at as strong. I have always been the person that holds it together for everyone else. I am the person that comes up with solutions to the problems. I am the one that has a backup for the backup plan. I have never been known to show public weakness. I'm known to those around me as competitive, driven, and an inspiration.

When you look at me from the outside, I exude strength and there is a light that shines when I walk into a room. I know this to be true. Even so, with all of this, I too have experienced moments of weakness. You may be asking yourself, "How can she be weak?" After all that I have experienced over the years, I am not sure we can call it weakness because there are so many layers to living life, but one thing is for sure and two things are for certain. Well maybe three or four. Whatever!

The point is that "Life Happened" to me. I did live through it, I learned from it, and I lost it. What I didn't know at the time, was that I was experiencing depression. In retrospect, I now know that I was not crazy. There was more to my story.

So, Girl, I'm not tripping, I'm DEPRESSED!

# Table of Contents

*"We must challenge ourselves to learn, simply by living."*

Chanita Foster

# Glossary

**Depression:** *noun* de·pres·sion \ di-'pre-shən , dē- \
(1)     an act of depressing or a state of being depressed: as
        a:      a state of feeling sad
(2)     a mood disorder marked especially by sadness, inactivity, difficulty with thinking and concentration, a significant increase or decrease in appetite and time spent sleeping, feelings of dejection and hopelessness, and sometimes suicidal thoughts or an attempt to commit suicide [1]

**Psychology:** *noun* psy·chol·o·gy \ -jē \
(1)     the science of mind and behavior

(2)     the study of mind and behavior in relation to a particular field of knowledge or activity [2]

**Psychiatry:** *noun* psy·chi·a·try \ sə-'kī-ə-trē , sī- \

(1)     a branch of medicine that deals with mental, emotional, or behavioral disorders [3]

**Therapy:** *noun* ther·a·py \ 'ther-ə-pē \
(1)     therapeutic treatment: as
        a. remedial treatment of mental or bodily disorder [4]

"*If you can find the strength to keep it real with yourself, you will always be strong enough to keep it real with others.*"

Chanita Foster

# Chapter 1: Real Recognizes Real

LET ME START BY SAYING that I am not a doctor! I have self-diagnosed often, and I have been called a hypochondriac a time or two, but I am not a doctor. I will say, that I am a person that likes to believe that I see things before they happen. I don't want to go off track by saying that I have spiritual gifts (that's an entirely different book, lol), but I am prepared for when LIFE HAPPENS! Say it with me — Life Happens. Life happens, and it happens to all of us at different times, and in different ways. Life doesn't care how rich you are or how poor you are. It doesn't care how beautiful or unattractive you may consider yourself to be. Life doesn't count rights and wrongs, what your religion is, or how much you pray or worship. Life has no consideration for if you are a college graduate or high school dropout. Your occupation can be that of a stripper or a corporate giant, you could be married, divorced, or single, but life will still happen to you. Whether you thrive in perfect health or you are living with a disease, life happens. Life doesn't concern itself with whether or not you grew up in a single parent home, or if your parents have been married forever. Whether you are an athlete or an entertainer, or even if you are the groupie that chases the athletes and entertainers. Whether you are gay, straight, transgender, or downright confused, we will all be faced with real life obstacles to overcome. Before I say another thing, I want to be crystal clear that real life happens.

If you are blessed to have lived on this earth for any substantial amount of time, you can understand what I mean when I say that life is a cycle of seasons. In each season, you will have both success and failure. Until I am certain that we are clear, I will continue to repeat that life happens. When life happens to us, and around us, we are at times caught off guard by the series of events that occur. And no matter how off guard we may be, there is one factor that remains consistent when life happens, choices. The simple fact that we still have the power in choosing how we will respond to the life that is happening is reassuring. You can choose to live through it. I did.

Simply put, this means that when life is happening, you get to choose how you keep living. You can harness all of your energy towards the positive things that occur. It is your choice. You can also choose not to give negative occurrences any of your energy. Consider the scenario of a crying child. When you hear a child cry, you are presented with two options for action. You can either allow the baby to cry, in hopes that he or she tires or begins to self-sooth, or you can take action to address the needs of the crying baby. In both scenarios, the crying will eventually stop. This is much like the daily occurrences in our lives. I think that we often forget that in many scenarios, the end result will be the same. We often forget that we have an abundance of power to choose what action we will take in a given scenario. We make our lives harder by spiraling out of control. In the instance of the crying baby, allow me to offer the scenario of the frantic mother. She may not be able to figure out why the baby is crying and in turn, gets frustrated or even panics. Many of us have been there. Most mothers eventually discover the ways to soothe their babies, and in life, we eventually discover the ways to be most positively impactful. Either way, every moment is a lesson that offers itself to us to learn through.

When life happens, we must learn to recognize it right away and discover the lesson in it all. Eventually, the mother learns to recognize each cry for her child and addresses it accordingly. Why don't we take this same approach to life?

Amidst these lessons, we must also learn to ask ourselves, a series of significant questions:

- What could I have done to change the situation?
- What can I do now to change the situation?
- Am I the direct cause of this situation?
- Could I have been better prepared for this situation?

This line of questioning is essential to the process of finding solutions. The beauty of learning when life happens is in the major epiphanies that occur. One major realization during this process, is that you have no control over people and certain situations. And as powerful as we are, it makes us even more powerful to know that what others do, how they think, and who they become, is outside of our realm of control. This means that you have removed all responsibility for the actions of others and transferred it to one person, you. Understanding that you can only control what you can control, is a major key.

Learning through life, gives you a different perspective on everything. If you acknowledge that every moment is an opportunity to learn, you will find that you are not bitter and can refrain from the "Why Me?" syndrome that we often fall victim to. While you are learning through it, you become eager to share what life is teaching you, and you recognize the lessons as blessings. If you are competitive like me, learning through it also means that you are keeping score because you want to win the challenge. You want to walk around with an "S" on your chest and a cape on your back because you were ready. You had a play book in hand to take notes and win. Let me give you a little hint — we never stop learning!

*"We must always look a battle in the face and tell it with authority to flee."*

Chanita Foster

# Chapter 2: You CAN Handle the Truth

LISTEN, WHEN I SAY that the truth will set you free, I mean that with every ounce of my being. Often times we are stuck in life because we aren't able to be honest with ourselves. We actually sabotage ourselves, when we deny this truth. I personally think that lying to oneself is a disease that is contagious. Trust me, I have lied to myself on many occasions. We all do. For most, it's easier to live a lie than to face the truth. There comes a time if you are lucky, that you grow. So, before we go any further, there are a few questions that I want you to ask yourself. Why, you ask? You bought this book for a reason. Either you went through a depression, you're going through a depression, or you aren't sure if you are in a depression. So, the next few questions are designed just for you. Some questions, you probably already know the answer to, but sidebar.... isn't it funny how we already know the answer to most questions, but we ask anyway to be sure. Let me tell you, I am the girl who has to call three friends and ask the question. Then, after that, I have to call three more people to poll the answer to make sure it's correct. All the while, I know the truth and the answer is always inside of me!

So, let's get to these questions!

What are some of the things that are said to you, or done to you, that trigger sad emotions?

_____

_____

_____

_____

_____

_____

_____

_____

_____

_____

_____

_____

_____

When you are sad or disappointed, how long do you stay in that state?

_____

_____

_____

_____

_____

_____

_____

_____

_____

_____

_____

_____

_____

_____

_____

Once you are sad or disappointed, do you know what you can
do to personally change your mood?

_____

_____

_____

_____

_____

_____

_____

_____

_____

_____

_____

_____

_____

_____

_____

Have you thought about taking your own life? If yes, what stopped you?

_____

_____

_____

_____

_____

_____

_____

_____

_____

_____

_____

_____

_____

_____

Have you experienced little or no desire to do social activities? If so, why?

_____

_____

_____

_____

_____

_____

_____

_____

_____

_____

_____

_____

_____

_____

Have you experienced increased anxiety? If so, for how long?

_____

_____

_____

_____

_____

_____

_____

_____

_____

_____

_____

_____

_____

_____

_____

_____

Have you had feelings of worthlessness, helplessness, or hopelessness? If so, for how long and what made you feel that way?

---

---

---

---

---

---

---

---

---

---

---

---

---

---

Have you had changes in your sleeping patterns? If so, what do you think is affecting you?

_____

_____

_____

_____

_____

_____

_____

_____

_____

_____

_____

_____

_____

Have you had changes in your weight? Weight loss or weight gain unrelated to dieting and exercise?

_____

_____

_____

_____

_____

_____

_____

_____

_____

_____

_____

_____

_____

_____

Do you find it difficult getting out of bed or leaving a certain area in your home?

_____

_____

_____

_____

_____

_____

_____

_____

_____

_____

_____

_____

_____

So, seriously, did you write the answer to the questions? If you didn't, stop playing and go back and do it. It's healthy. Plus, as I stated, the truth will set you free. If you answered YES to most of those questions and needed about six extra pages because you had a lot to say, chances are you have been depressed, are depressed, or are heading towards depression. Again, I'm not a doctor, but here is what I know. If I had been asked those questions when I first started to feel those emotions, I could have, potentially, saved myself a trip down the road of depression for the extended amount of time I was in it. Just use the internet if you don't believe me. Google! Google questions to answer and see if you are depressed. Then you will find that I have my Ph.G. — my doctoral degree in google, because I googled it before I wrote it to make sure I was spot on.

This is the bottom line, you can handle the truth! Determining the truth is also the equivalent to winning the battle. Most of us don't allow ourselves to have a full shot at winning because we are too afraid to face the truth. Facing the truth is equivalent to clearing the fog from the bathroom mirror and looking deep into the reflection to see ourselves for who we truly are. And whether we decide that we like what we see, or we don't, coming face to face with the truth is more powerful than we can fathom. We have to be willing to do the work to get to the truth.

*"We should never judge others on the choices that they make if we are unaware of the options from which they had to choose."*

Chanita Foster

# Chapter 3: They Say Hindsight is 20|20

HAVE YOU EVER HEARD me say life happens? I thought so. Let's get into it. You see, most often when life hits us, it shakes us in ways that we can never be the same. That was the effect that my first major hit had on me. I remember waking up, but I was still somewhat in a state of slumber. It was almost as if I wasn't really awake because a real-life nightmare had manifested in my life. Some even seem to think me telling this story is disrespectful because I was married when it happened. To the contrary, I think that if I would have addressed it sooner, it would not have been such an integral part of what I would later learn was my depression. Trust me, the part about caring what other people think is coming. So, sit back and wait for that too.

I grew up in Detroit and Oak Park for most of my childhood life and while this isn't an autobiography, I have to shed light on this journey for it to all make sense. My high school was in a suburb called Oak Park and was named Oak Park High School. I was a phenomenal student, when I wasn't getting kicked out of class for talking too much, and I was an even better athlete. Like most, I was trying to rush my way through high school. As an adult, I admit that sometimes I wish that I could go back. And even though many moments are a blur, from not remembering teachers, to forgetting the names of some of the people that I spent time with, there was one moment in particular that changed the trajectory of who I thought I was and who I would later become.

I remember the day like it was yesterday. Our suburban school was going to compete against a Detroit public school. I am still uncertain as to why, because during my three years there that had never happened. We were part of the Suburban Athletic Conference (SAC), so the likelihood of us playing a Detroit Public School was out of the norm. In retrospect, I'd like to think that it was all a part of God's plan in leading me to the next phase of my life.

It was football season and I was a cheerleader. How I became a Cheerleader, I don't know because to this very day I can't even do a cartwheel. I had just come off the field from performing at halftime when I heard a voice.

"Hey," the voice said, with a very deep tone. When I turned to look, not only was the voice unfamiliar, but so was the face. My first thought was, "Who is he and why is he talking to me?" I returned the greeting and kept walking, until I heard him say, "You are the most beautiful girl I have ever seen in my life."

Come on man! Y'all know I stopped dead in my tracks, right? Why? Because in high school I was not it! Glasses, braces, goofy, loud, not shapely, and annoying come to mind. So, outside of Carl Brown breaking my heart by kissing a girl in the B wing (you Oak Park alumni go tell it because that's another book. Your first heartbreak!), I wasn't getting much action from boys. So, yes, I stopped and we talked and I liked it. Because again, this is not an autobiography, I'll fast forward past the smiles, laughs, conversations, and yes, my first kiss.

On my birthday, during my senior year of high school, I traveled the forty-five minutes it took to get to his house in Detroit from my house in Oak Park. I made this trip every single weekend from the time we met. Shout out to my mom, who was actually the driver. I know I didn't appreciate it at the time. She would drive forty-five minutes to drop me off, then drive forty-five minutes home, only to repeat this when I needed picking up. For those of you with a calculator, that's three hours of driving. Writing that just made me realize she was/is the real MVP! OK, so, back to the birthday!

When I arrived at his house, there were no gifts, not even a card. Remember, I said it was my birthday, right? I remember him reaching into his top drawer (Yes, I was in his bedroom. At the time he shared it with his mother and little brother, Walter. Just focus.) When his hand appeared again from the drawer, he was pulling out a shining object the size of a quarter. He grabbed a paper clip and worked it out so it would hang on my necklace as a charm. I will never forget the words he spoke.

"I don't have any money. Actually, I don't have much of anything. This is the only thing that I have in my life that has any value and I'm giving it to you."

Baby! I was in tears like the man proposed to me. I never looked at the shiny object to see what it was. I just knew that it was mine and since it was all he had, it meant the world to me. It was the first thing he had ever given me.

I went to school the next day and when I walked into my biology class, my teacher, Mr. Bloomfield took one look at the shiny circle thing around my neck and almost passed out.

"Is that a State Championship medal?"

I'm like, "I don't know. My boyfriend gave it to me."

"What's his name?"

"Robert Traylor," I reply.

He turned completely red and yelled, "Robert Tractor Traylor?"

"No, just Robert Traylor."

This man then took the liberty of throwing up countless numbers and percentages, but I was confused. Basketball? He never told me he played basketball! I talk to this boy every day and he never mentioned basketball. Most of you are thinking I knew, but I didn't. So please, hold your thoughts about me being a groupie or what not in high school because in my Sunshine Anderson voice I'm singing, "Heard it all before." FOCUS on the story people.

I needed answers, so I raced home and beeped him! For you new generation adults, that's a little black box that we had to send a message to with limited characters and no emojis, leaving us to be creative with just numbers. After which, we had to stand by our house phone (the kind with a dial tone) and wait for them to call back.

OK, time to fast forward again. Yes, he played basketball. Yes, he was Mr. Basketball for the State of Michigan. Yes, he signed to the University of Michigan and on signing day I sat at that table in a daze because I knew life as young love was over. And finally, yes, he played in the NBA. But none of his athletic career was a factor of my story or depression.

What was a factor was he was the FIRST person to teach me self-love! He accepted those braces, glasses, flat booty, no chest, and Payless shoes. For a woman that matters! And, if you go back far enough in your memories, you will remember the first man, outside of your father, that made you feel beautiful. So that was major!

The second thing he taught me was VALUE of relationships and words! See the VALUE was in our relationship, not possessions.

"I don't have money, but you can have everything and anything that is of value to me!" he said.

That was life defining and it has carried with me my entire life. See, you can interview any of my ex-boyfriends, or even friends, and they will tell you that our relationship is not built on material things or opportunity, but on the value, that they brought into my life and the words spoken into my soul.

So, imagine this, fast forward through seventeen years married and six children and we are still amazing friends. So much so, that he invited me to his wedding, which I politely declined. (Are you kidding me? Robert, you really thought I was going to sit at your wedding. Hilarious!) I was in a great season in my life.

Remembering again like it was yesterday, I was in Kroger, on Cascade in Atlanta, Georgia with the kids and my phone rang. My baby sister Joi asked, "Where are you?"

"At the store with the kids, why?"

"Call me when you get home," she said and hung up.

My phone rang again, only this time it was Craig Urquhart, a childhood friend whom I didn't speak to often. He said, "Where are you?"

I replied, "At the store, why?"

"Call me when you get home."

At that point I knew something was up. Call it God or the fact that Craig calling tied it together for me, but my first thought was, "What did Robert do?" See Craig and Robert played AAU Basketball together, so most of our conversations were filled with old basketball stories and athletes. My heart, mind and spirit made a natural jump right to Rob.

I gave my daughter, Amber, the basket to push and I went to my virtual best friend that has all the information from stock market tips to gossip. Google! I googled Rob's name, but nothing popped up except old stories about tax trouble he'd had, so I felt relieved. I left the store and made my way to Wendy's. I was in the drive thru when my sister called again.

"Where are you? You need to go home! I'm not going to talk to you until you get there."

I pulled off, not even getting the kids food. My sister remained on the line. I was nervous and the whole ride home I was convinced that someone was either hurt or dead. I knew it deep down inside. When I pull up to the gate, I could see my husband, George, standing in the driveway. My heart dropped. Someone was dead for sure. When I pull in the driveway my sister said, "Are you home?"

"Yes!"

"Is George outside?" she asked.

"Yes!"

The words that came out of her mouth next seemed to reach me in slow motion. "ROBERT DIED."

I don't remember what happened for the next few weeks. The longest relationship I'd had, outside of family members, was gone. How do I process that? What made it difficult was that I was married. Married and happy. So, trust me when I say, it was hard for most people to understand how I could be upset about another man dying.

Let me help you out. See, in the story, I said that we shared something that most people don't. VALUE! It wasn't about what he could do for me financially. Again, please be honest, most relationships are built on what another person can add to their life financially. In my mind, at the time, I felt that no one could see me in the way that he saw me. Not the well put together, educated, successful person that I am now, but that girl with the braces and the payless shoes. Remember, our relationship started in the rawest form.

So, my first thoughts encompassed the loss of that feeling of security and acceptance. Because when I didn't feel pretty enough, or good enough, one conversation with him would remind me that I was worth it, just as I am. I am worthy of love and that was priceless.

I know it sounds foolish, but when life happens you aren't always thinking with your rational mind. In addition, I felt like I lost pure honesty. Honesty at its rawest form. He NEVER lied to me. (Well, not that I know of.) That meant something to me.

For those of you still thinking, "Poor George," stop it. He was fine, for a few reasons. First, he respected our friendship. I wasn't intimate with Robert after we broke up. When I'm done, I'm DONE! Second, our friendship was open. There was nothing to hide because we were friends. Lastly, once Robert passed George said, "There is no competition with a deceased person." Yep, go ahead and call George the bomb.com.

After the funeral, I couldn't pull it together. As hard as I tried, I still had countless moments of breakdowns. Every time life would hit me like a ton of bricks, I wanted to pick up the phone and call him. I remember sitting on the side of the road, talking out loud, praying for the opportunity to hear his voice one more time. It never happened. He never spoke back, and as things began to change in my life, it got harder and harder to shake. Would this feeling of emptiness ever go away?

See, that was the beginning. If someone had said, "Go get help," then maybe my process of grieving would have been different. History has told us to be strong. The stigma of getting help handicaps many. Popular opinion alone handicaps people. I was left to grieve in secret because I wasn't sure if grieving was appropriate. So, if my situation was complicated in my mind, imagine the people without a complicated situation who have a hard time grieving. Lack of understanding can be the formula for destruction.

Remember those questions? It was asked, "What are some of the things that are said to you, or done to you, that trigger sad emotions?" My answer was, "When someone asks me why am I still grieving." It would make me angry! Piss me off! Mess up my day! That question would be a reminder that he was gone. It made me mad that people felt like they had the right to tell me how to feel. I felt like I was being judged. I thought it was an unfair question to ask or state and ultimately lead me to where I began to answer the question with this response, "He was in my life for over seventeen years, so I guess I will get over it in seventeen years!"

I didn't know there was a time frame on grief. Also, seventeen years is a long time to be on this emotional roller coaster. What I did learn (remember when life happens you have the option to learn), was that there is a time frame in which you should get help! Lack of help leads to depression and destruction. I'm not sure if I will ever stop thinking about Robert. What I do know is that I now recognize my emotions when it comes to questions about when and how I grieve. I no longer let it affect me to the point of shutting down, getting mad, or losing it.

*"Before you assume, you should consider asking."*

Chanita Foster

# Chapter 4: According to Me

AFTER SURVIVING MY first big hit in life, I felt like I was out in the middle of the ocean treading water. I was tired, mentally, spiritually, and physically, but I was waiting for help to arrive at any moment. I wasn't drowning, but I knew that help needed to come sooner rather than later before I drowned in the mental sickness called depression.

It amazes me now, that I knew that I needed to catch myself from something, but I wasn't quite sure of what. Have you had one of those moments when you keep asking yourself, "What's wrong?" I was in that mental and emotional space. Right when I felt like I heard a helicopter coming from a faraway distance, meaning I was almost out of the space of grieving Robert and attempting to find people with value, I then came upon my SECOND hit! George Foster was retiring from football.

Before we begin this journey of the second hit let me clarify some things about me, which you might not know or find interesting. First, I'm only going to give you my part as far as my feelings and what I was going through when George decided to retire from football. I'm not sure if you can ever imagine, but it was life altering. The end of anything is tough, mentally and emotionally. Depending on what is ending, it can be life altering financially. George's story is his own, and if he indeed decides to tell it one day, I want it to come from his thoughts, his views, his perspective, and his words. Not everyone is willing to share things that are personal to them. So, it's HIS story left for him to tell. Reason being, there are always three sides to every story, and multiple perspectives, so I owe him that respect. Second, because I have lots of books inside of me and if you think for a moment that I am not going to write a book about my experience and journey as a wife in the National Football League (NFL), think again! That book is coming. As a matter fact, there should be countless handbooks and manuals on how to be a wife in the NFL. Indeed, if there were a book with the TRUTH, lots of players, wives, and families would be saved from exactly what we are about to talk about, transition and depression!

Now, focus and let's get back to the second hit. George was retiring from the NFL and to be honest, when it was first mentioned, I was fine with going through the process. I had already heard from countless wives that retirement was going to be a process, so in my mind I was thinking, "We got this." I knew it would be an adjustment for all of us, including the children. With the financial alterations, I knew that I wouldn't be able to spend at the same rate if I wanted to continue to create generational wealth. I had begun a budget a long time ago and trust me, you only really need one, hot new purse a year. These days I wish I could take some of those purses back to the store and get my money back! Side note ladies, purses and shoes are bad investments and the really expensive shoes hurt! For those of you that don't know, the acronym, NFL, does not stand for National Football League. It actually stands for Not For Long in most cases! But, believe me when I say, there were a few things that I didn't realize and therefore didn't prepare for. Baby, let me tell you, when they retired George Foster from the NFL, they retired Chanita Tennelle Ellis Foster too!

It wasn't until George retired from football and someone went to introduce me in public, that I fully comprehended what was REALLY happening to our lives. We had relocated back to Atlanta, aka Hotlanta, and began to call it our final home. I was just beginning to feel settled and was making new friends in the city, when one evening I was invited out by a young lady (no use in naming her because we still end up in the same room from time to time and y'all would snitch and tell her I was talking about her in my book.) Once at the event, I was feeling the new Atlanta scene. The people kinda had that down south hospitality that you just can't teach. So, I welcomed the warm smiles and friendliness.

The young lady I'd gone with went to introduce me and she said, "Oh my gosh. I want to introduce you to my friend Chanita Foster. She is married to NFL player George Foster who plays for..."

She paused, waiting for me to fill in the blank because she wasn't sure what team to say he played for. So, still smiling and preparing to stick my hand out to shake hands with a warm welcome greeting, I replied, "Oh, he doesn't play anymore. He retired."

Listen, the look that came across their faces, you would have thought that I had spit on their Mamas! You know that look of utter disgust. The look you make when you can't believe someone ate your leftovers out of the refrigerator. The look you make when your children ask you for a morsel of your last bite of food. That is the look I'm talking about!

There was a short pause as they looked at each other and then she began to speak again. "So, he doesn't play football anymore?"

"No, he retired after nine long years. He had an amazing career with the Broncos, Lions, Browns, Saints, and Colts." I was giving them the whole George Foster NFL career run down when I realize their looks of disgust weren't evaporating.

Do you know that the woman she was introducing me to walked away? Like for real, turned and walked away! I'm talking full RuPaul, cross one leg over the other, swing your hair, arch your back, turn and walk away. She didn't even look back. I figure, if you are going to turn around all dramatic you should at least look back with it. She didn't. With a disgusted look of her own, the young woman I came with, faced me as if she was ready to fight and said, "Why didn't you tell me your husband retired before we came here? I wouldn't have invited you. Are you kidding me?"

Listen. Are you kidding me lady? I was standing there like I'd just been punked! Where are the cameras? Is Ashton Kutcher about to come from around the corner, because this can't be real life. So, I tried to hold it together and I said, "What do you mean you wouldn't have invited me? What difference does it make if he plays currently or use to play?"

Do you know, with a straight face, she looked me in the eye and said OUT LOUD, "I only invited you because I thought your husband played in the NFL and you would be a good fit for this crew, but since he retired I'm not sure if they will accept you coming to events and hanging out with us. We have important things going on in our lives."

I was at a loss for words. Like, really... lost for words and I talk... a LOT! Was she basically saying I can't sit with them? Did she say they have important things going on? No disrespect to the NFL, but when did playing football become important? My heart sank deep. It was taking everything in me to hold back the tears. I wanted to turn into the Detroit girl. The Eastside girl who played in the street on Algonquin. I wanted to cuss. As a matter of fact, writing this I want to cuss! Why? Because I realized I had LOST myself in those nine years. I had no personal value to people anymore. They were saying Chanita Foster, but what they were really saying was Chanita Foster, George Foster's wife that was the first-round pick in the NFL Draft in 2003 for the Denver Broncos and he is famous and important because of that and if you aren't attached to the fact that he was a professional athlete, then we don't want anything to do with you.

I need to clarify for you why I am upset. It isn't just the loss of value, it is about the deconstruction of who I was at this point in my life and the outright disrespect. We have to address this, because when moments like that happened, it made me feel like I was a bum, a groupie, as though I wouldn't have made it in life if I hadn't married an athlete. Let me help you understand. You see, I like to help people, right? At the time of this foolery and disrespect, I was Chanita Foster, a college graduate, with multiple degrees. I had a career in sports management that started in Chicago, Illinois, under the mentorship of Keoki Allen. I had worked with and worked for athletes such as Mike Finley, Jerry Stackhouse, Ron Artest, Greg Buckner, Marcus Fizer, Shannon Brown, Tim Hardaway, Stephon Jackson, Jason Terry, Karon Riley, and Jimmy Farris just to name a few. I'd raised over five million dollars in funds for multiple non-profits. I was a Board Member on multiple boards, some in which I was the youngest. I owned a clothing line called, Wife Material Custom Jerseys, where I designed and made the uniforms for the Atlanta Falcons and Arizona Cardinal cheerleading teams. I had worked for a Fortune 500 company on mergers and acquisitions. I can go on and on, but let's be clear, this was all before I married the NFL player that they were placing my value on. Oh, and it gets even better. I earned six figures before I got married! So, I'm confused. All that to choose from and you want to lead with, she's married to NFL player George Foster? Are they crazy, confused, or haters?

From that day forward, it was a rolling snowball effect of hurt from people. I couldn't digest that I wasn't worthy anymore because he didn't play football. I was still Chanita Foster, right? Not! You have to realize that people place value on what you can do or potentially do for them. Because I was in it at the time, football was just George's job and how he got paid. I didn't understand. Going to a football game was what fed my family, so no big deal. However, to everyone else, it was seeing someone that they idolized and admired. Getting autographs from players after the game excited them, but to this day, I don't understand the reasoning behind it. I just see it as a name on a piece of paper. Again, no disrespect, but this was my life.

So, I did my best to try to process this new reality, but it wasn't working. The people around me didn't know me and therefore placed no value on me. As such, the only thing I felt was pain, which only became more exacerbated when facing the fact that there was no more Robert to call for reassurance. Remember, he was the first person to teach me value. He accepted me a hundred percent as is, and I didn't have that anymore. (I know what you are thinking. Why not talk to George? Ummm, hello! If I am getting treated like this, imagine what he was going through.) Let me paint the picture for you. Membership has its privileges. I didn't make the rules, so don't get mad at me for pointing them out. Cutting the line, loaner cars, free cell service, floor seats, exclusive parties, free shoes, free samples, not waiting for a table, etc. It all disappeared.

I'd tell myself, "Chanita pull it together. You are a good person. Show people you are the same person." My attempt at showing my value, however, was an epic fail! Let me explain why. Always an explanation, right? I was standing in the bathroom, naked, looking at myself in the mirror. Have you tried it? Stand in the mirror naked. Your view of yourself becomes different. Some people pick themselves apart, critiquing everything they don't like, but I was standing there looking for answers. When you stand there long enough, you begin to see things and ask, "What is that? For me, it was the diamond football helmet around my neck and the six-carat wedding ring on my finger. Those were the two things I could remove that attached me to him, the NFL player. I was headed to a dark place and I was mad at George. I wanted to be free of what was making me feel like this. It was time to take off the diamond helmet charm and my wedding ring.

Some of you will say, "Why remove the wedding ring?" Well, wait for it. Just, wait for it. One day, I decided to take a trip to the store. I remember the day, like it was yesterday. I can't remember the name of the store, because that would be a name I would tell you. I did my normal looking around. It was a clothing store, so I remember looking at dresses. Am I the only person that doesn't like trying on clothes in the store? I began to walk towards the dressing room, debating with myself if I was going to try on the clothes or not. I saw a few sales attendants along the way that walked towards me and then walked past me. When I arrived at the dressing room, they kept asking if they could send someone to help me. Each person I encountered said, "Give me a moment and I will send someone over to assist you." That was enough for me to be over trying on clothes. Yep, that was my excuse. I didn't want to try them on anyway, but I was feeling some type of way.

What was different? Why were they treating me this way? My hair was combed, makeup was flawless, and my clothes were neat. Not that it should matter, but I know I was carrying a name brand purse. Purses and shoes are my weakness! I'm saying all this, so you understand that I didn't look like I was homeless and ready to rob the store, so why not help me or ask if I needed help? I left the store aggravated that day, though I wasn't sure what I was aggravated about. Was it that I didn't try on the dresses, or that no one would help me? Key word HELP. Was I expecting that store to change how I was feeling? I was tripping for real! In addition, I began to question my financial situation. Was God sending me a sign that I shouldn't be shopping? I knew we were on a budget, but a dress? See, when you are going through it, you are looking for signs in everything because you're seeking confirmation that what you are doing at the time is correct. You are looking for a small victory in something because in life you are losing. Well, let me not say you, because again, I'm not a doctor. So, I will stick with when I, Chanita Foster, was going through this, I was mentally all over the place. I wanted help, but help for what? I was misplacing aggression on a dress and a store attendant. What I knew was that I, Chanita Foster, needed a victory that day. I felt like I was losing and as a former athlete (that's right, no one mentions that I was a full scholarship athlete, or that I was an Academic All American. My entire athletic career is trumped due to the fact that George played in the NFL) I don't like to lose!

The next morning, I was still feeling crazy. Now, I don't like being called crazy, but I was beginning to feel crazy with my emotions all over the place! So, I did the same thing I did the day before. I walked to the bathroom, took off all my clothes, and stared at my naked body in the mirror looking for answers. I stared long and hard. With tears rolling down my face I whispered, "HELP."

I couldn't figure it out. My children were home, so I was trying to pull it together, but the tears wouldn't stop. At one point, I remember laying on the floor naked. Then, I had a super mom moment. Do you know what a super mom moment is? If you are a mother, it is that moment that you want to completely fall apart, throw in the towel, and you receive a certain vision or thought of your children and you snap out of it. A super mom moment won't save you every time, but most of the time. This was one of the times that my super mom moment saved me! I hopped up off the floor thinking of my children walking in with me laying on the floor naked and crying. Plus, I knew they were hungry for breakfast. Team Foster doesn't play about their breakfast! So, I got up. I got up off the floor and I actually smiled a little bit. Why? Because you remember I was looking for small victories. Me getting off the floor that morning, was enough to count as a small victory.

Once off the floor, I decided to put my ring and chain with the diamond football helmet back on. I'm not quite sure why, but I knew I felt like I was missing something the day before. Since I had been wearing both of those things for over nine years, maybe there was a mental connection to the items. Maybe, they were kind of like my security blanket. How many of you are like me when it comes to a wedding ring or something you wear every day? I promise, I could be twenty minutes from the house and if I look down and I don't have my wedding ring on, I will turn around and go all the way back home to retrieve it. If I had a meeting and I left my ring, I promise you, I would be late. I am going back home to get my ring, period. I have even had it shipped to me, if I flew somewhere and left it at home. SMH.

That morning, I fed Team Foster, who by the way, walked in the bathroom after I had pulled myself together. Shout out to mommy powers that morning for saving me. After breakfast I headed off to the store, but I had my guard on. I had prepared all the rude, slick stuff I was going to say to people if they didn't help me. They were short, one liners to make a point, like, "That's why you work this $7.00 an hour job... because you are rude!" and "You will never get anywhere in life with your funky attitude!" or "I didn't want your help anyway."

You know that people who hurt, hurt people right? Since I was hurt yesterday, I was armed and ready to hurt everybody right back. Isn't it funny how I practiced all the mean, slick stuff in my head? Who else does that? Come on be truthful. You are hurt or mad and you want someone else to be hurt or mad, so you practice how you are going to get them. If you are still saying you have NEVER thought that, congratulations, because you might be part of that rare 3% — the nicest people in the world. I, however, was with it that day and in full battle mode. Anybody could get it, because I was mad and hurt! But, something strange happened in the store that day. Everyone was so friendly and helpful. Are you kidding me! Was I tripping? I felt like I was in the twilight zone. Then I had one of those moments when I was standing still, like in a movie, and everyone was moving past me really fast, so much so that they turned into a blur. You know what I'm talking about? I was certified tripping, but don't judge me.

What was different? I had one of those moments where I started touching and looking at myself, as if looking for something on me. You know, almost like when you smell something foul, and you start checking yourself. "Is that me?" Pull it together Chanita Foster. (Side note. This was the phase when I really was talking to myself, often. I needed to hear myself, because I didn't hear anyone really speaking into me. Remember I felt I lost value.)

I finished my shopping, and this time I made sure I didn't leave empty handed. I was also proving to myself that I was OK financially. I was buying something out of that store, period. Whether I wanted it or not, I was buying something! My silly self, grabbed some extra random item for sprinkles on top, and walked to the front of the store. I waited in line, not speaking to anyone. I placed my things on the counter when it was my turn, and when I finished, I looked up and that's when the sales associate said, with a southern twang, "No one who worked here wanted to interrupt your shopping and ask, but what team does your husband play for?"

How did she know he played football? Is she the Feds? IRS? You know the space that I was in, I started thinking all kinds of stuff. So, I politely said, with my teeth tight together, in a calm tone, "What makes you ask that? Why do you think my husband plays football?" But, what I really wanted to do, was snatch her up for asking about my husband, or football. I'm still mad from yesterday, but because I'm a mother, I refrained from slapping this girl, because I didn't want to go to jail.

Now, remember, I was in battle mode. So, what I wanted to say next was, "So you think my husband is a football player, because I am black, and carrying a nice purse, and wearing nice shoes?" Oh, I was ready baby? Pure coolness was in effect. I was in full trip mode. Don't judge me!

She says, "We saw the diamond football helmet hanging on your chain and your ring is so beautiful! How many carats is it? I want a ring that big. Can I see it? Who did you say he plays for?"

I wanted to die! Damn! First off, I didn't say he plays for a team, because he doesn't! Oh, I was MAD! Second, ring up my stuff, so I can go before I throw it at you. At least, this is what I was thinking. I was heated! People didn't want to help me in the store, or be friendly, unless they saw a money value on me? I had to be attached to an athlete for good service? That was all it was the day before? Because the helmet was made of diamonds, and my ring was diamonds, that was what was important? Being attached to money, is, in their opinion, a demonstration of value. That famous saying, "People meet you on the outside first," is not a lie! She didn't know that I was a good person, and had accomplished a lot. She didn't know that I feed a thousand children in Swaziland, Africa, every single day, or that I cashed in my children's 529 college fund, to build a school in Africa. She didn't know that my son and oldest daughter are adopted, and that I started a foundation called Beyond The Game, (BeyondTheGame.org) to serve the widows and orphans of Swaziland, Africa. Nope! My value to her was dollars, not my personality and my heart. I was done. It never occurred to me to wonder, "How could that girl know these amazing things about me?" It's not as though I was wearing a Beyond The Game t-shirt, or a shirt reading, "Please respect me, because I am more than a NFL wife, of a player that just retired, and in my spare time I like to save the world."

Now, after writing that, maybe we should all walk around with a shirt saying how we want to be treated! That way, when you are going through a bad season, or depression, people know how we expect to be treated, or need to be treated. Cool idea, right? I might have to look into that. That would probably save a lot of people from losing their religion and cussing people out! You know, I'm laughing while I'm writing this, because I know some of y'all are thinking you are going to buy a shirt tomorrow, and you know exactly what you are going to put on it.

Over the next few weeks, other emotions started to creep up on me. I almost resented George. It wasn't his fault, but it was his fault. I started saying stupid stuff like, "Why did you play football anyway? Isn't it too early for you to be retiring? People retire when they are old. You aren't old! What is your problem man?" Thank God, I was saying this stuff to myself and not him, but I was saying it nonetheless. And guess what? I was saying it out loud, talking to myself. I'd just start singing too! Remember that song, "I talk to myself"? I know, I know, I'm old, but there was this song, and it became one of my theme songs at the time. The song was by an artist named Christopher Williams, entitled "I Talk to Myself". The lyrics spoke to my heart. He spoke of talking to himself because he was lonely to the point of no return. The lyrics paint a beautiful picture of a person who is on the verge of breakdown from the mounting pressures of life. In the song, he expresses how lonely he is, because there is not one who would understand his feelings. The basis for the feelings was insurmountable pain from being used by others, and longing to be understood. I could relate so heavily to the lyrics and they resonated in my heart.

That is one heck of a theme song to be walking around singing. Shout out to Christopher Williams for the assist in my season. How many of you know that you have a theme song that plays in your head? It can be gospel, rap, R&B, whatever, but you do have a theme song for each season of your life. Here is the kicker. You have to pay attention to the words of the song. The words will determine what season you are in, and sometimes, explain why you are in it. If you aren't lying to yourself, (some of you are lying to yourself for the entire time you are reading this book) then you will realize, you really do have a theme song. Now, think about the lyrics, or go download them so you can read them. Nine times out of ten, you are going to be like, "Man that's deep!" Yep, I told you so.

There have been a variety of theme songs in my life. I've even adopted a theme song for my entire family. DJ Khaled's, "All I Do is Win," has become synonymous with the sentiment that I want my family members to act from. If I can encourage them to believe that they are winners before the world has an opportunity to tell them anything different, I believe that I offer them a fighting chance at success. We can all take note of such a mindset. I wish you could hear me singing this song! It always makes me enthusiastic about life and what's to come. In all of your spare time, you should visit my good friend Google and look it up for yourself. Now that I think about it, you're probably already singing along, if you know the song that I am speaking about. Can you imagine that playing in my head all the time? It's true. I have the t-shirts for it ironically. My shirts say, "Win Baby Win." I once asked John C. Maxwell, "What is the theme music that plays in your head?"

He said, "For the first time ever, in all of my career, I do not have an answer."

Can you say amazeballs!? I tripped up John C. Maxwell, so I know some of you are tripping! So, get yourself some theme music, and make sure the words tell your story. I feel bad for whoever is reading this book and decides their theme song is "Panda." Yep, I am laughing out loud again. Google the words to "Panda," then you will know why I am laughing!

Let's get back on track. I was mad that I had lost my identity. I took off my ring and that stupid diamond helmet for the second time. I know people speculated as to why I was walking around without my wedding ring on, but I was gone by then. Who cares! I replaced that diamond helmet with a cross on my neck. Even though I wanted to believe that I was a child of the most high and that he had value for me, outside of being the wife of a football player, I no longer had the strength to believe.

Today, I know better. I know that along the way, God has always had a plan for me, just as he does for you. There are times when life's haze makes the life happening in front of you so unclear, and this was one of those moments for me.

Today, if you go to my social media, @chanitafoster, you will see the cross that replaced the helmet around my neck. I pretty much NEVER take it off. It helped save me. I eventually learned what truly redeemed me, and of course, I'm going to share it with you, but you have to KEEP READING! My entire attitude began to change completely, from the simple act of removing the football from around my neck. Even those around me, who still respected me enough to talk to me, couldn't understand what was going on during my spiral. Trust me, there's more. Now, some might say, "It's no big deal. He retired from his job, move on," and others might demand, "Girl, stop tripping." But my reply was always, "Girl, I'm not tripping, I'm Depressed."

*"Don't be so certain that you can't lose it all. If you don't learn through it, losing everything is possible."*

Chanita Foster

# Chapter 5: As A Woman Thinketh, So She Becomes

BY THIS TIME, I'm trapped in the closet. No, like really trapped. Like, start singing R. Kelly, trapped in the closet. Only, I'm not cheating, and there is no Mr. Big, but I am trapped! (If you are lost with the entire trapped in the closet reference, just Google it.) So, I'm not literally trapped with a chain, lock, and big security guards standing outside of the door, but I am trapped, physically just as much as mentally. There were days when I just couldn't bring myself to get up and move my legs. I wanted to get up. I wanted to break free. I wanted to be in a different position, and I knew I had the ability to do so, but I couldn't. I don't mean that my legs were broken, or weighed down. My legs weren't tied together with navy seal knots, or locked with a passcode that was confidential, and only the United States Secret Service could crack it. It was more like I was trapped like the kid that fell down the well, and the entire world watches as it takes hours to free him.

Clearly it was mental. I don't think people understand that almost everything that we do in life, starts with our mindset. Our mind determines if we can, or if we cannot. Both answers are correct, because of the power of the mind. Now of course, there are certain times that it is physical, and you have to build your mind, body, and soul.

Let me give you an example. When I was in high school at Oak Park High, I played varsity volleyball. I was a middle hitter and right-side blocker. My job was to watch the ball while it was in the air, time it correctly to jump, and block it from coming on our side of the net. Here is where it gets even better! You not only have to watch the ball while in the air and moving fast, you have to time it correctly personally, and you also have to time it correctly with a teammate! If you don't time it correctly while the ball is in the air, you will both jump at different times, and the ball will go between the hands of both of you. I left out the part that when you jump, you have to know where your feet are, so you don't step on each other. That's a lot to remember, right? I might as well have been a quarterback named Jake Plummer, who is my favorite quarterback of all time. Just follow me.

There was one particular game during my senior year that I remember like it was yesterday. The play started with the ball on the other side of the net, so we were playing defense. I saw the ball in the air, and I made sure to follow it with my eyes. My footwork was on point, and I moved into place, planting my feet for a strong base to jump. I jumped in the air to block, but one thing happened in that moment that had never happened before. I forgot the position of my feet on the way down, and I ended up landing on my teammates foot! Did I just break my ankle? I didn't just break my ankle, did I? Did I at least block the ball?

To this day, I can't remember if I blocked the ball, but here is what I do remember. The pain was like nothing I had ever felt before! Now that I think about it, it hurt more than pushing out one of my kids. Seriously! Pain, like giving birth with no drugs, kind of pain.

I remember Coach Gibson running over and he said, "Stop crying, and get up now. Don't you embarrass me." He was a man with posture. A very proud man, who was hard on us. The reason he carried himself with such a strong, confidant posture was because volleyball was a predominantly white sport, and we were an all-black team. So, when we walked in a gym, we were meant to keep our heads high and play hard. It was killing him that I was crying, although, I was really hurt. He said it again, this time through his teeth, like when your mother is super pissed at you, but she doesn't want the world to know that she wants to cuss you out and beat you on the spot. "Chanita, get up now. Stop crying, and get up. Don't you embarrass me, and don't embarrass this team."

I wanted to get up with everything in me, but I couldn't do it! I tried again. I closed my eyes and put both hands on the floor. I pushed with all my might, but the pain was too much. Finally, with anger in his eyes, he picked me up and carried me off the floor. He walked right past the bench, with my entire team looking, and out to the bus! He was mad! I was handed a bag of ice to put on my ankle and left to wait on the bus until they came back when the game was over.

The bus was completely silent. I don't know if we won or lost. Actually, I take that back. Let me brag a little. From 1989-1995, we never lost a game. So, I guess I just told my age. The bus took me directly home, rather than to the school, and I remember them carrying me into the house and placing me on the couch. Before he closed the door, Coach Gibson said, "Call me when you get up."

After he closed the door, tears began to stream down my face. I was hurt. I didn't want to disappoint him, or my team, and I was embarrassed. All I had to do was get up, walk off the floor, and make it to the bench, so the trainer could look at me. I couldn't be hurt that bad, or they would have taken me to the hospital instead of bringing me home, right? Wait. Did the school bus just bring me home?

I lay on that couch, not moving for a while because no one was home. After a time, I began to think, maybe, I can get up and walk. Maybe, I just wasn't trying hard enough. Isn't life like that sometimes? You think, if only I try just a little bit harder. So, I swung my legs around from the position I was laying in, so I was sitting straight up. I took a deep breath, planted my feet firm, like when I'm getting ready to jump and block a ball, and with everything I had in me, I pushed myself in a forward motion and stood up. Well, in my mind I stood all the way up. The key word being mind. I screamed at the top of my lungs and hit the floor with the crash of a Floyd Mayweather knock out. I was done! Stick a fork in me. Call the cleanup crew. Finished. Complete. I really couldn't stand up. I lay on the floor crying until I cried myself to sleep. Question. Is it really crying yourself to sleep, or is it that you are in so much mental and emotional pain that you pass out? I'm super serious! Because when you cry that hard, your breathing pattern changes, and you get light headed, so that's a real question.

I don't remember who found me, or who got me up off the floor, but I'm sure if I had to guess, it was my mom. Like most good mothers, she was not always there when you wanted her to be, but right on time to save you! Shout out to my mom.

See, that was a moment where my mind and heart wanted me to get up, but I wasn't physically ready. I began rehabilitation, so I could get off of those crutches quickly! It was mentally killing me that my body wouldn't do what my mind was telling it to do. After a few weeks, I tried again. Trust me, I was nervous. Once you feel pain like that, you don't want to feel it ever again in life, but I was ready. This time, without me giving you all the dramatics because after reading this far you should know I'm extra dramatic, I was able to stand up, but I was still in pain. I was standing, but it hurt!

Why did I tell that story? Because, while I was trapped in the closet and I couldn't stand up, it was like that ankle. My heart, mind, and spirit were broken. So, I couldn't just stand up and walk out! As much as I wanted to, I couldn't do it! I needed rehabilitation.

The definition of rehabilitation is: the act of restoring something to its original state.

How many of you need a little rehabilitation? To be restored? See this was a combination moment of physical and mental rehabilitation for me. Just because I could stand up and take a step, didn't mean I was healed. Standing up was just the first part.

Once I rehabilitated my ankle, I still couldn't play in any of the games. I could show up, but I wasn't able to play. That was me in the closet. I could stand up, and get out, sometimes even go into the kitchen, but I wasn't cooking. I was there, but not in the game. You know how, when players aren't playing that most of them don't wear a uniform? Well, I want you to imagine me not wearing a uniform in this thing called life! Honey, I was getting out of the closet, but I wasn't taking a bath, or putting on clothes (aka my uniform). Do I have a witness out there? How many of you have had a moment, when you were going through it, and you just couldn't figure out how to get dressed and you found yourself wearing the same clothes for days?

So, there I was trapped in the closet. Then it began to get even better! While trapped, those people that were closest to me began to come over my house to visit, and tried to have real life conversations with me. Yep, you heard me correctly. My friends and family members actually arrived at my house and I was in my closet. No one asked a single question. They would just come, and talk to me in the closet. So, I ask you, was I crazy, or were they?

Although everything had changed about me, in a physically and mental capacity, nothing had changed for them. It was like my volleyball teammates when I got hurt. I was hurt and they were not. Because they were getting dressed physically for practice, putting on a uniform, practicing on the court, and playing in the game, everything was fine for them, but I was hurt! In their mind, I had no reason to be hurt or upset with them, because I was still there at the game in the physical sense. My friends and family, like my teammates, were going about their everyday lives, and because I was still living and breathing, to them I was in life too. Only I wasn't! I was on the bench, unable to play, hurt both physically and mentally.

The mind is a powerful thing! What is your mind saying to you? What are you reading or watching? By the time I got into the closet, my mind was telling me that I wasn't worthy, that I had no real friends in the world, that the world no longer accepted me, because George didn't play anymore. But it didn't stop there. My mind told me that I wasn't a value to people anymore, that being only a mother and a wife wasn't a real job. It then went on to convince me that I was too old to get back my career. All of that, every word, was on replay in my head, and it played over and over again, every single day.

I remember my friend came over and sat there in the closet talking to me for hours. I watched her move around in the closet, touching things. She picked up shoes and admired them. I realized she wasn't talking to me, but really just talking. I promise, I could have been anybody, anywhere. She didn't need me to respond or reply. What few questions she asked, she ended up answering herself. Yep, she was talking to herself. I told you that everyone talks to themselves; even people that aren't depressed and sitting in the closet.

It wasn't until she started taking clothes off the hanger that I became aggravated. Only, I wasn't upset for over anything logical. I wasn't mad that she wasn't talking to me, or disappointed that she hadn't made eye contact. Heck, she didn't even notice that my tracks were hanging out of my hair, and that was definitely something to be angry over. I can go on and on, but what I was irrationally upset with, was that she was pulling the clothes out and looking at them, and then putting them back in all the wrong places! Was she crazy? Why would you pull a black shirt out from where all the black shirts are, and then put it back where the red shirts go? Why would she do that? See how irrational my thinking was? But my thoughts didn't stop there. I became convinced that she was doing it on purpose, and the only reason she showed up at my house was to make me mad, because she knew I was broken. It was so obvious that she was never really my friend, and she most likely sat around talking about me to other people. How had I ever liked her? She was there to take and not give. I believed in that moment that I hated her and that she knew I hated her.

See how crazy I was thinking? All of those thoughts were moving around in my head. She began to try on my clothes and shoes, while I sat on the floor staring off into space. Did that heffa just put on my shirt? Baby, I had to be broken, because one fun fact about me is that I don't like anybody in my clothes. Not even my mama. I'll give it to you before I'll ever let you borrow it.

On a side note. Do you know how many friendships and relationships are ruined over borrowed clothes? Like, seriously. Social media has made it even worse. For example, let's say that you let your friend borrow your shirt. A week later you don't have your shirt back. So, you go on Facebook and your friend has posted a recent picture wearing your shirt, again. Of course, you are a little irritated, but she will bring it back. You still have faith. Now, it's two months later and you are on Instagram and she is, once again, in your shirt! Bulls eye! You call her up, and tell her she didn't return your shirt. Here is how that conversation goes.

"Girl what shirt are you talking about? I don't remember borrowing a shirt from you."

Instead of you telling her she is trifling for wearing your shirt three times, when you've only worn it once, you politely send her a screenshot of it in order to refresh her memory.

Once she receives the photo, she says, "Girl, first of all, I forgot that I borrowed that cheap, ugly shirt. Second, if you wanted your shirt back, you should have called, and asked for it back. But, no worries. I will put your funky shirt in a bag and bring it back to you tomorrow. Oh, and just so you know, I will never ask to borrow anything from you ever again. Trust me!"

And that, Ladies, is why I never allow people to borrow my stuff. See how your shirt is suddenly funky and cheap? Oh, and my favorite part, about how you don't have to worry about them borrowing anything from you again. They act as if you are the problem, and they are doing you a favor. So nope! I don't like people in my clothes.

So, getting back to my friend, who had joined me in the closet. After a while I couldn't take it! She just kept putting on my clothes. But, was I really mad about the clothes? Come on Chanita! Tears began to pour down my face. I couldn't stop them. I couldn't get the words out. I wanted her to get out of my stuff. I wanted her to leave. After trying on another of my shirts, she turned her attention to me. The crazy thing is she saw me crying, and then turned like she didn't see me. She went back to my clothes and I lost it. I was sobbing. Shocked, she put the shirt down she was holding. Might I added, this fool put it down on the floor. The crazy thing is she put her clothes on and looked around for her purse. So, she messed up my closet, and now she just wants to get her stuff and leave. Forget the fact that I am sobbing on the floor. Once she was all together and had her purse, she finally turned to me to speak and Baby, it was powerful. I'm talking State of the Union with President Barack Obama, kind of powerful. Like, when you are home, sitting with a bowl of popcorn, waiting for Scandal to come back on. Like, sitting in the audience of the Black Girls Rock award show. (Y'all know I'm going to win a Black Girls Rock award, right?) Like, receiving a donation for BeyondTheGame.org, so I can continue feeding a thousand children in Swaziland, Africa. It was that powerful! To this day, I can't believe what she said to me.

With a straight face, she asked, "Girl, what's wrong with you?"

Did she just ask me what's wrong? Like, for real? What's wrong with me? I wanted to smack her. I wanted to punch her in the face. I wanted to scream at her. All that and a bag of chips, but I couldn't. I was trying to speak, and the words just wouldn't come out. I was out of breath from crying so hard. I took a few deep breaths and managed to get out, "I don't know."

She looked at me like I was acting like a dumb blonde. Rather quickly, that look changed to one of frustration, then confusion, then annoyance, and finally to a look of sympathy. Her various facial expressions actually caused me to crack a smile, because it reminded me of the Michael Jackson music video, "Black or White." Do you remember that video? The faces change with different emotions.

"Girl, you don't know? How you don't know what's wrong with you? Get up! Get up right now, and stop crying. Get up off the floor, and let me borrow this shirt. You are tripping!"

Did this dummy just ask to borrow my shirt out loud? This can't be my life right now. God, please help me. Please help me! This time, I didn't even respond, but in my mind, I was saying, "Girl, I'm not tripping, I'm Depressed!"

Before you move on to the next chapter, I want you to take a moment to reflect upon a few more questions. I know for sure, that what we think and what we remain focused on, determines what will happen in our lives. I was focusing on a pattern of thought that would later prove to be self-destructive. This was not my goal but I had not gained the insight to recognize that my thoughts controlled my feelings and therefore, my actions. Sometimes, I don't think we even realize what types of thoughts consume our minds. I want you to think about it. Like, seriously, think about it. Don't play now. Answer these questions for real — with your heart.

1. What is something that you think about daily?

_____

_____

_____

_____

_____

_____

_____

_____

_____

_____

_____

_____

_____

_____

_____

_____

_____

2. What is the happiest thought that you have?

_____

_____

_____

_____

_____

_____

_____

_____

_____

_____

_____

_____

_____

_____

3. What are you holding onto that you should probably let go of?

_____

_____

_____

_____

_____

_____

_____

_____

_____

_____

_____

_____

_____

4. What do you think about yourself?

_____

_____

_____

_____

_____

_____

_____

_____

_____

_____

_____

_____

_____

_____

_____

_____

5. What do you believe others think about you?

_____

_____

_____

_____

_____

_____

_____

_____

_____

_____

_____

_____

_____

_____

_____

_____

_____

6. Would you say that you love yourself? Explain your answer.

_____

_____

_____

_____

_____

_____

_____

_____

_____

_____

_____

_____

_____

_____

_____

_____

7. Why do you matter?

_____

_____

_____

_____

_____

_____

_____

_____

_____

_____

_____

_____

_____

_____

_____

_____

*"You could attempt to save yourself. The choice will always be yours."*

Chanita Foster

# Chapter 6: Who Can I Run To?

AT THIS POINT, I'm sure you understand that I wasn't tripping, I was depressed! Like, really depressed. In the closet, you remember? But, just so we're clear, while I was depressed, I didn't call it that. If you are going through it or made it out, you probably still don't say out loud, "I am in a depression," or "I went through a depression." It wasn't like I walking around saying I was depressed. I just knew something was wrong, really wrong, and I couldn't fix it. Like ninety percent of the world, I did not recognize what I was going through, and those around me could not understand, comprehend, or label what it was either. That's why most people hear the statement, "Girl, you just tripping."

The depression statistics are staggering. According to the U.S. Centers for Disease Control and Prevention (CDC), one in every ten American adults say they have depression.[1] According to the National Institute of Mental Health (NIMH), 6.7 percent of American adults have MDD, or major depressive disorder, during an average year.[2] The Depression and Bipolar Support Alliance states that depression affects more than twenty three million Americans every year and that it is the most common serious brain disease in the United States.[3] Numbers from the World Health Organization estimate that about 350 million people have depression globally.[4][5]

We have to be honest, though. A lot of us really do trip. Don't act like you don't know what I mean. We all have character flaws unique to us that people accept despite the fact that the behavior is oftentimes unacceptable. I know you have heard, "Auntie Betty is always trippin'! Just leave her alone."

When we display that behavior, the natural response becomes, she is trippin'! No one thinks to ask that person if something wrong? Why do they feel a certain way? Why do they act a certain way? It is deemed as trippin'!

Although this isn't an urban book, I used the urban word, "trippin'," so let me make sure you are clear on the definition. The urban dictionary defines "trippin'" as, "When someone is overreacting, or getting all bent out of shape over something small."[6]

The keyword that stands out in the definition is "overreacting." That word makes it difficult for a person on the outside to understand why you are depressed because it minimizes and generalizes what you are going through, what you are about to go through, or what you just came out of. The truth is, depression is never an overreaction. When you are in a depression, going into one, or just coming out of a depression, nothing about that time is trivial, and at no point does it feel as if you are making a mountain out of a molehill. Depression feels like a ton of invisible bricks, resting on your shoulders. When depression takes over, you question yourself. You become paranoid about how those around you will view who you have become.

I can clearly recall conversations with Mrs. Goldberg, my counselor at Roosevelt Middle School, in Oak Park Michigan! She was my safe place, and we spoke every day.

"Mrs. Goldberg do you think I'm crazy?"

"No, Honey, I don't think you are crazy. I do think that you need to speak to someone that can give you more insight on how you feel and why you feel that way."

In my mind, I thought she was calling me crazy, but I trusted her. I remember she said she was going to call my parents and talk to them about it. You know that wasn't going to go over well with my parents, right? You are going to call Billy Dent, and tell him his family needs to go see a counselor? OK, Lady. Have at it, but I'm not sure how this is going to turn out.

My prediction was right. My dad wasn't with it, and my mom was trying to understand, but this is where I KNOW for a fact that my parents loved me unconditionally, with everything in them. Why? Because we ended up at a therapist office. They love me! They really love me. I grew up knowing that love is when you don't want to do something, or quite understand something, but love propels you into action. That's what my parents did for me. I knew it was hard for them and not necessarily something that they believed in or wanted to do, but they did it regardless.

For the first few sessions it was just me and the therapist. I remember she was a lady, and just like in the movies, there was a couch in her office. I had the choice of sitting up or laying down. Which one do you think I chose? Y'all know my overly dramatic self, had to lie on that lady's couch, so I could get the full effect! Baby, I was there for the entire experience. I was able to get so much off my chest as far as emotions, and I was beginning to learn what I had control of and where to place my feeling. It isn't my story to tell, but just know that there was a lot that was going on in my household at the time. I don't think that people understand that children are smarter than you think. Children, see all and hear even more. There are a lot of people out there putting their children in adult situations because they are privy to the adult conversations. I most certainly was, as a child. So, I was carrying a lot. When you love your parents and family, you want everyone to be happy and everyone to get along.

There came a time when the therapist invited my mother and father into the sessions. When I say I was nervous, I was nervous. I was in there sweating like a sinner in church! I was praying that my dad wouldn't cuss this lady out. He is good for a good cussing out if you say something crazy to him.

"Dear Jesus. Please don't let Billy Dent cuss this lady out. She is here to help. She doesn't know he is crazy. Order her steps Lord, and allow the words that come out of her mouth, be words of respect. Please allow everyone to leave the room without anyone being smacked. If someone gets smacked in here, I know this lady has the police on speed dial, because she deals with crazy people. Lord she doesn't know. She doesn't know that we are a dysfunctional family that likes to yell and curse to get our point across. Cover her father. Allow us to touch and agree. In Jesus' name we pray. Amen."

I promise you, I kept saying that prayer over and over again while this lady was talking to them. I kept staring at my dad's face. Was he cool with what she was saying? My mom was smiling this fake smile she was good at. Sorry Mom. You have a fake smile and it looks fake, for real. Don't kill me. I'm just being truthful with these nice people that spent their hard-earned money on this book.

It was finally my turn to talk. Deep Breath Chanita. They can't beat you in front of this lady. Well, they can beat you, but they don't want to go to jail, so just do it. Say what's in your heart. I began to speak. At first, I spoke slowly, making sure it was safe. Once I caught a glimpse of them looking at me with intent to hear, it was on and popping. I began to share everything that I had been sharing with the therapist. I mean everything. I completely threw up all my bottled-up feelings. All the stuff that you know damn well you can't say to your parents, I said it. I was in full snitch mode. I was a lightweight, telling all the stuff that would be questionable to the law when it came to parenting children. I even broke down food choices and where we went on vacation. I was giving it all to them! When I was done, the room was silent, and the calm scared me. I thought, "I'm going to die. They are going to kill me. Well, they aren't going to kill me in front of this lady, but when we get home, they are definitely going to kill me." The silence broke when my parents began to address what I said. Only they didn't speak to me, they spoke directly to the therapist. At this point my parents were completely ignoring me. I wasn't there. They didn't even make EYE contact with me.

Do you know that the only thing they heard, out of everything I was talking about and venting about, was that I wanted a dog? A dog! Because I was so emotional and crying and mentioned the dog, that is all they heard. Dog! I remember them saying over and over, in the office that we weren't getting a dog. Then, the therapist spoke. To be honest, I had checked out by then and was crying. I wanted a dog. I really wanted a dog. OK, I get it, you didn't hear anything, and my rant was obviously pointless, but after all that I couldn't even have a dog? Even the therapist was saying I should have a dog. So, what was the problem?

We left that day, and I was never taken back to the therapist again. As a matter of fact, we never spoke about our session. We also never spoke about me having a dog again. I think I need to call my parents and ask what was up with the no dog thing.

So, why did I share that story with you? Because I wanted you to know that even though someone may love you enough to want to help you through your depression, they still might not get it. They may be unable to process why you feel the way you feel. I was a kid back then, so I was under my parent's management. They get everything I have as an adult, because they tried, but ultimately, they didn't get it in that situation.

From the time that the idea of the therapist was introduce to them, my parents were closed off. They were like most people when it came to therapy, "What is the purpose of having this person involved in your life?" Now, add that to the fact that I was only a child. "Why do we have to go to a stranger and tell them our problems?" My parents aren't alone in their thinking. This is the general consensus, for most people, on the idea of therapy and therapists. So, here is the point. We already know that what you're going through is hard for everyone to understand, but you also have to be aware that most will not want to be part of your seeking help. Don't let that deter you. Help is needed, so don't give up on finding some.

Depression is a real disease, and people are suffering every day. I was suffering and in pain! It takes a strong person to go to sleep and wake up and decide that something is wrong with you and want to fix it. I seem to think I'm one of the strongest people on this earth! Don't we all think that? That no one is as strong as we are or been through the things we been through. Even with all my strength and resources, I still went through a depression, and I was not strong enough to get out by myself and seek help. So, I feel like if you are anything like me, you are blessed because this could have ended all bad.

I remember laying on a bathroom floor, arms stretched out, legs wide like when making a snow angel, with a gun in my hand. I knew I wasn't going to shoot myself, but it felt good. I promise, I wasn't going to shoot myself! I lay there and I thought about dying. Have you ever thought about dying? Have you tried to close your eyes and silence the world out? You lay completely still, trying not to move. I was just like that.

My brain went through a list of morbid questions. Who would come to my funeral? What would they dress me in? What songs would they play? What color would my funeral flowers be? I could see it even though my eyes were closed. I could hear crying. Then I began to cry. Death is associated with hurt and pain. I was hurting. I was hurting bad! Why was I laying there? I opened my eyes and looked at the gun. This is stupid, Chanita. You know damn well you aren't going to shoot yourself. Then I thought about my children. I could hear the sound of their voices. I could hear them laughing. Then I could hear them fighting. Why are they always arguing with each other? Then my thoughts shifted. Who would take care of my children? Who would love them like I love them? Then I saw the faces of the people I knew loved me. If I die I would affect them too. I didn't want them to feel what I was feeling. I thought about Robert. Memories of us came to mind — all the good, bad, happy, and sad times. But he was gone! He had no control over dying. He probably didn't think about the thousands of people that would mourn him around the world. He didn't think about the affect it would have on me. He was my first hit and with that hit I needed help! Major help, from a person with a degree!          There was a knock on the bathroom door. I had to hide the gun, quickly. Can you imagine if I had opened the bathroom door holding a gun in my hand? Whoever was on the other side would have been like, "Girl, why you holding a gun in your hand? What's wrong with you? Girl, you are trippin'!"

I would have had to explain, "Girl, I'm not Trippin', I'm Depressed!"

*"If I fall down, life happened. If I indeed get back up, I chose to live."*

Chanita Foster

# Chapter 7: When It All Falls Down

I'M IN THE CLOSET. We know I'm depressed... Super Depressed! We know Robert died and I haven't mourned. We also know that George retired from the NFL after nine years and because of that, the world retired me. Despite knowing all of this, I still felt lost. Did I mention that I gained about ten pounds? OK, let's be honest, more like fifteen, but who's counting? Now, let's add people!!! Did you know that people have the power to affect you to the point of making you depressed?

The world that we live in has incorporated social media. This addition is affecting millions of people. Oh, the power of a post and the thumb thugs! Do you know what a thumb thug is? Well, a thug in real life, is a violent person, or a person that does harm. So, a thumb thug is a person that is violent with words, and they do it with their thumbs! Basically, they type their hate and live to disrupt people's lives. They call it personal opinion, but all of their words are aimed to destroy and break people down. I think thumb thugs are the worst because you can't get them! You can't talk to or argue back with them because they are sitting behind a computer or cell phone somewhere, creating this madness. Social media and people have the power to shift the mindset of others. I know they did for me! They contributed to the closet situation I was in. We can start with social media and then get to the people part.

Just like all of you, I like social media. No, I take that back. I love social media! Now, let's be clear, I'm not a Facebook person. Some people should be paid a salary for the amount of time they spend on Facebook. I learned a long time ago that Facebook has the ability to stop income producing activity in my life! What do I mean by income producing activity? Well, activity that aids in my producing income, money. Anything that disrupts me making money, I'm not for it at this point in my life. Facebook does not pay me, Chanita Foster, for my use of the application. Does it pay some of you? I'm serious, because I have family members that live and die by Facebook.

I used to get on Facebook and find myself on there for hours! For hours, I'd go from page to page looking at other people's lives, good or bad. I remember a particular day, after my baby was born, sitting on Facebook for eight hours straight! Are you kidding me! I would just sit there and stare at the screen, searching on and for people. People that I knew and didn't know. I started stalking, yes, I use the world stalking, people that I was no longer in contact with, not realizing that we weren't in contact with those people for a reason! But, I found myself back on their pages time and time again. So, I learned quickly that Facebook wasn't for me. Yes, I have a page. Everybody has a Facebook page, right? As a matter of fact, I have multiple pages that look like I interact on it daily. But, just know it's really only connected to my Instagram page, so I am posting on Instagram, and it goes to Facebook by default. But, let's get to what I call the devil, often times called, Instagram!

Instagram is both a gift and a curse! We have a love hate relationship. We are like sisters. Some days I love and often days I hate. I started off loving it! Seriously, as a photography major I loved the pictures! I loved how the pictures would tell stories. I loved that I could show my friends and family members what was going on with my children lives. Instagram allowed me to expand my business. I was able to post my projects and what I had going on. IG allowed me to grow Beyond The Game

(Beyond The Game.org). I was able to get sponsors for the thousand children that I feed every single day in Swaziland, Africa. The power of the hashtag allowed me to connect with people all over the world! So, in the beginning, I thought that IG was better than sliced bread.

How many of you know that people don't really post who they truly are, or what they are really going through, online? I know that now, but I didn't know it back when I was going through it. So, how did Instagram, something that I had grown to love, add to my being in the closet, depressed? Let me tell you.

I would roll over in the morning and not pray or brush my teeth, but check Instagram! I know I'm not the only person! Trust me! Raise your hand high, right now, if Instagram was the FIRST thing that you did every single morning. Some of you won't even get your kids a bowl of cereal until after you've checked Instagram! I did a poll on this and it applies to the majority of the people on IG. You want to see what it is that you missed while you were sleep. Have you ever woken up in the middle of the night and reached for your phone just to check Instagram? Again, I know I'm not the only one. Crazy, right? But, I would get on it and scroll through. Now, let's look at Instagram through the eyes of a person like me, going through a depression. A person that is broken, lost, and hurt. Suddenly, Instagram looks a whole lot different.

I first would see athletes. Athletes never bothered me before, right? First, NBA players bothered me. Looking at NBA players made me sick to my stomach. They all reminded me of Robert! When I think about or see a basketball, it reminds me of Robert. They were alive and still playing. Key word, alive. I resented them. I was mad at them. So, I had to unfollow them — all of them. A sport that I once loved, I now despised and hated. Hate is a strong word, and I hated the NBA, the players, and anything that had to do with the sport. There were no exceptions. To this day, I only follow Stephen Jackson, whom I use to work for. Trust me, I worked for plenty of NBA players, but for some reason I'm OK with following Stephan. Shout out to Stak5, aka Stephan Jackson. Thanks for supporting me. Oh gosh. Why did I just do that? Now everyone is going to feel like I should shout out to them too. Man, just focus!

Then, let's get to my NFL family. I was never a true NFL fan, but over the years, I had fallen in love with some parts of the game and some people. I would log on Instagram and see all of the wives still in the game. They were still going to the games, dressing their children in team colors, and cheering for their husbands. I didn't have a team to cheer for. I couldn't cheer for my husband. I had no reason to put on a jersey, or take selfies on the field or by the locker room. That sounds shallow and stupid, right? I didn't have a favorite team anymore. My favorite team was the team that was bringing a check into the house, to provide for my family and the children in Swaziland, Africa. So, I have been a Bronco, Lions, Brown, Saint, and Colt fan! But, during this time and depression, I didn't have a team.

Sidebar. If you follow me, then you know that I call my family, Team Foster. The reason I call us Team Foster is because when I was going through it, I felt like I was losing it all. I didn't have a team to cheer for, but I had them! We are Team Foster. In this game we call life, we will win together and lose together. How well the game of life goes for me is dependent upon us living and working together as a team! Each one of us has a role in order for us to win as a family. All of us serve different positions on the team and each role is important. All of us will be in the game a hundred percent all of the time. As long as we are stuck together and playing together we can make it! We also have a no trade rule. You cannot be traded off Team Foster!

Although, you will often hear me tell my children (I promise I tell them this often) when they act up, that they can go to another family or get traded to another team. Don't judge me, it works! It's hilarious when my children get in trouble in public. They will scream out, "Please Mommy. Please, I don't want to go to another family. I don't want to go on the trading block. I will be good, just don't send me to another family!" Do you know how people in public are looking at me thinking this lady is about to give away her children? Hilarious. It works, thought. At least I'm not beating them in public. I'm just scaring them. Try it with your kids. It works.

So, Team Foster was my team and that's who I had to learn to cheer for and who cheered for me. Cheering is important. I know I said I wouldn't mention George, but I want you to imagine this. From the time George was a young child, he had someone cheering for him. "Go George! You are the best. You can do it. Great job. You are so awesome." Now, I want you to imagine that he goes to sleep one night and when he wakes up, it is silent. No one is cheering for him. No one is saying his name. Can you imagine that? Silence. Now, imagine the same thing for me and my children. All the people that were cheering and celebrating us, had stopped. It was quiet. Now you know why we are Team Foster! Now you know why Team Foster is important to me! I have watched other people coin the saying, without truly knowing or understanding why I came up with it. If you see other families using it, help them out and tell them to read this book. Shameless plug. Lol.

Once I unfollowed a bunch of wives, and NFL players, and fans that I grew to like over the years, I was left with people. Prior to social media, it was hard to tell how people really felt about you. Meaning, you had to wonder if they really liked you enough to invite you to things, support you, or involve you. If something happened and you weren't involved or invited, you wouldn't find out until after the fact. That's if you even found out at all. Why? Because it wasn't documented, so you didn't know. But, on social media, you catch all the shade! I realized all of the people that used to invite me to their houses, parties, baby showers, weddings, and events weren't inviting me. I would scroll through and see the get togethers that I wasn't invited to, and it hurt. It really hurt. The visuals of them laughing and smiling. People that I use to spend a great deal of time with. Is this real? Is this life?

Then, everyone just looked so happy! Super happy! Like the commercials when everyone has the big smile with their mouths wide open. You know the laugh and smile I'm talking about. The one that looks like you have heard the best news in your life! So, everybody is just happy? No one was having a problem? No one had someone die? No one else's husband was retiring? No one was going through a transition? All I saw was happiness! Life was exciting for them and they made sure they showed it. Everyone was still going to the store, balling out, and I was on a budget. Instagram life looked good and I was going through it! How many know that I was living the truth in the closet, in a depression, while they were living a LIE? A big Instagram lie! People aren't who they post themselves to be! That's real talk! They weren't always happy! They were going through it too. Maybe not to the extent I was, but something was going on. It wasn't until I took a social media break that I realized it was all smoke and mirrors! Don't be fooled like I was with these Instagram lives. So, now that I'm out, I laugh when I scroll past some people's post because I know that no one's life is perfect.

Now, to the people part and back to the validation thing. So, I wasn't valid because George didn't play anymore, and because I didn't have the newest bag or shoes? Oh yeah, it got real for me. I was out of the make-believe circle. Remember, at the time, the circle mattered. Let's be very clear. Where I am right now, I don't care about the circle, square, or triangle, but in the midst of it, it mattered! I'm not worried about if you are going to let me sit at the table because of Total Life Changes and Stormy Wellington. I'll just buy the table (yep that's another book). People can make or break you sometimes. Some people that I thought were my friends, proved me wrong quickly. I had friends that I bonded with on each team, and they let me know that once I was no longer a part of the team, I was no longer a part of their lives. They were women that I had laughed with, cried with, won with, and lost with, and now, they wouldn't answer my calls. I lost a Godmother to one of my children with the change of a team!!! That's deep.

When I relocated to Atlanta, I thought I'd made new friends! Not! Let's not call them friends either. You remember that introduction at that party at the beginning of this book? It was a snowball effect. No reality TV relevance or NFL attachment and it was over for me! They can blame it on whatever makes them feel good. Trust me, many of them are reading the words on this page because they bought the book to see what I am talking about. Yes, I am talking about you! You stopped being friends with me, not because I was loud, not because I walked in the room like a storm and took over conversations with passion, not my long story telling or my long way of answering questions, not because I said what I felt and didn't do fake! You stopped being friends with me because I couldn't get you a football ticket, because you couldn't go on the field, because you couldn't use my last name as leverage in business and personal situations, because I didn't have on the new shoes or my name on the waiting list for the new purse.

Whew! I just took a deep breath! Yes, it still bothers me sometimes. I gave you me! I gave you my love and prayers, my smiles and ideals. How many of you gave to people and then were hurt by them? When you feel used and let down it hurts. Trust me, I understand because I have been there too. But don't worry, people hurt people. You aren't tripping. You are Depressed!

As mentioned, often times, others will deem your behavior as overreacting. Especially crying. To most, tears are reserved for something devastating and should be reserved for such occasions. How many times have you heard someone say, "Is that really worth crying about? Why are you crying? Stop crying for no reason!"

I know for me, I am not a big crier, but while I was depressed, I would cry. I would cry a LOT! As a matter of fact, I would have the good cries. You know when you cry, but it starts to get real ugly? When you allow the snot to stream down your nose and it mixes in with the tears? Baby, that ugly cry is the best! It's the type of cry that when you pull it together, your entire shirt is wet from the tears and snot because you couldn't be bothered with a tissue. That's when you know you are in a good cry. Please don't act like you don't know what I am talking about, and please don't act like you haven't wiped your nose on your clothes during a good cry. If you have not wiped your nose on your clothes during a good cry then pray to the lord above and say thank you because you really haven't cried yet. For those of you still saying, "I don't know what she is talking about. I haven't!" It's OK, but remember I told you that the truth will set you free!

A good cry needs a good soundtrack. What am I talking about? Sound effects. See, when you get into a good cry, you need sound. Imagine a wounded animal, like a dog, mixed with a cat, mixed with a mouse. (Well, at least that's what I think I sound like.) As the tears are following and the snot is running, the sound track is playing. If you are anything like me, you get loud with it. You don't care who hears you. Partly because you are probably in a closet or locked in your car and feel like you are in a fully enclosed recording studio. Each sound that comes out are the words to your drama, hurt, damage, and unforgiving pain.

As I said, I would cry a lot and I promise it was over small things. No one around me understood what I was crying for. "Girl, why are you crying? Stop it! Pull it together. Girl, you are Trippin'."

The lines between normal trippin behavior and depression behavior become blurry. Really blurry! So blurry that no prescription from an eye doctor could make it clear for the eyes of others. Nothing allows them to see down into the depth of your soul, or ease the pain in your heart and spirit.

The definition of "trippin'" also says, "getting all bent out of shape over something small."[1] Well, when I was in it, nothing was small! I was depressed! Everything was big. There were no small things in my opinion. It all mattered. Every single thing in my life mattered emotionally and mentally to me, and any little thing had the potential to set me off. I'm talking about things like, running out of milk. Who has ever had a set it off moment about some milk? You are depressed, mad, and aggravated again, not knowing why, and you finally get hungry and now you're out of milk. See for me, in a depression, I either didn't want to eat at all, or I felt like I was just completely starving. Well, in the starving moments, I probably really was because I know for a fact that I would go days without eating anything.

Sidebar. A visual of depression that you can now look for in friends and family members is severe weight loss or weight gain. Just think about it. The average person doesn't just choose to gain an extra thirty pounds unless something is wrong — really wrong. Pay attention. If you see someone gain in excess of twenty plus pounds in a month or so, something is terribly wrong! The same applies to weight loss. So, pay close attention to those around you. It's an easy sign to watch for visually. OK, back to it!

Sure, I knew that some of the things that were happening to me in my life at the time were not enough to send me over the edge, but it wasn't a single thing that was pushing me over. Me becoming depressed was a combination of things, happening to me over a course of time, with no resolution, no closure, and no solutions. If you really look at that time and what I went through, the issues hitting me hardest were mostly things that I had no control over! Isn't that the worst? No control! No control is losing it all! Seriously. Some control freaks go crazy for real. No control is like tell the quarterback he can't run the play. Huh? He is the quarterback. That's what they do. They run plays to execute the victory. I need to run the plays, don't you?

It wasn't until AFTER my depression, I learned that we can only focus on the things we can control. Chanita Foster, you can't control things and you can't control people. As much as you want people to act and be what you want them to be, you do not control them. It doesn't matter how much time, money, or love you give a person, that does not constitute you being able to control them. So, get it out of your head that you can control people with your actions. The only person, or situations you can control are the ones that deal with you! If you want to get technical, we all know who is ultimately in control, right? Don't get me to preaching a sermon on trust in the......

As I began to look back over the series of events that had taken place in my life, I realized that the small things that had gotten me into the closet and into my depression, were not small to me. They were all major hits. Hits that would alter my life forever! I now realized that I needed help at each one of those moments. I was waiting for the magic wand. I was waiting for someone to come save me from myself. Have you ever heard the saying, "No one is coming to save you"? It's true! No matter how much you believe it, the only person capable of saving you, is you! What kind of help did I need during this time? I needed it all: mental, emotional, and yes, spiritual help as well! As stated in the beginning, this is not a religion book, but just know that spiritual help was a significant piece of the equation, but that's another book in its entirety. I should have used a therapist in each of the situations that were life altering and life changing.

I know going to a therapist, for most, is considered taboo. I'm not personally sure why it is taboo, but it is and it's sad. Going to a therapist is needed, not just for people going through a depression, but for anyone that feels like they have an issue. At the beginning of this book I said I would only tell my story because it's not fair to tell other people's story. It is theirs to tell, at their own time, in their own way. I'm going to stick to that, but I want to share with you an example. Let me apologize to my mother and father in advance because this is not a shot at them, but an example to help give clarity and shed some insight on what I went through personally. Since it happened to me, and I went through it, I think it's only fair that I can use it as an example. Right? Send me an email later if you think I shouldn't have used it as an example.

When I was younger, I used to talk to a counselor named Mrs. Goldberg, who worked at Roosevelt Middle School in Oak Park, Michigan. Shout out to my middle school memories. Mrs. Goldberg was my safe place at that age. I could go to her and tell her everything, and I mean everything. Sometimes, she would even let me skip class. Listen, don't judge this lady for letting me skip class, OK. She was helping me. (Focus!) Now, imagine me as a child! I talked ten times more than I talk now, and ten times faster! Hilarious! My nickname from my father was, "Mouth of the South." Really? Why would you name me the mouth of the south, Dad? The funny thing is that we didn't even live in the south. I'm going to ask my dad why he called me "Mouth of the South" when we lived in the Midwest. I'm sure he is going to say, "Who cares," and that the point was, "I talked a lot and too much!"

After talking to Mrs. Goldberg for a while, she stated she was getting concerned. One day when I ended one of my hour-long stories, which sometimes turned into a rant, Mrs. Goldberg said I needed to go to a therapist! She said, "Chanita you know I love you right?"

"Yes, I know. Are you about to kick me out of your office?"

She smiled, "No, I'm not going to kick you out my office. I do, however, think that you need to see a therapist."

Back then, I didn't realize that Mrs. Goldberg actually was my therapist. My daily conversations with her, were just what I needed. Far too often, we deny ourselves the power of being able to speak our true thoughts in a non-judgmental environment. Had I known the power of it then, I'm sure that I would have recognized the tremendous results that manifest from this concept. Today, I know for certain that we can all benefit from therapy, especially those of us who are in danger of being depressed. If I can tell you one thing, I can say with certainty that therapy works. Let me say it again, therapy works. If you find that you are straddling the fence about it, DON'T. There are few words that can describe how seeking professional help can change your life. I would venture to say that even if you are not on the brink of a depression, therapy can prove to be beneficial. The bottom line is that we all need someone to talk to. Just trust me when I say, don't miss the chance to save yourself.

*"People serve a purpose in your life. When that purpose ends, let them go."*

Chanita Foster

# Chapter 8: Change Your Circle, Change Your Life

I REALIZED COMING OUT of my depression that some of the people in my life no longer served me for growth. This is a hard one. We have friends and family members that we love so much, that have been with us through thick and thin! They weathered the worst storms in our life, but are they helping you grow? It is something to evaluate.

Change your circle, change your life, is as real as it gets! Stormy once said, out loud, "If you hang around five broke people, you are going to be number six!" I took that statement from that day because it is TRUE! Look at the people in your life. Are they make you richer, smarter, or bringing you closer to God? If the answer is no, then we have work to do.

It was as hard for me to transition into changing my circle, but then life changed and I became happier! I would meet a person at the coffee shop and ask, "May I have your card?" Only to find out they were the CEO of a company and lived in a massive house! Or I'd meet the Cheer Mom, who just happened to be the wife of a huge pastor! I'd never hung out with the cheer moms, but this one was different. I remember when I first saw Cleo Oliver. She had on a pair of drool worthy boots, which I took a picture of and sent to my friend Frank Pompey, who knows all the fashion. Frank texted back, "You don't want those boots. They are over $1000!" When I saw her again, she had a Gucci purse, which I had never seen. I sent Frank another picture. "Girl, that is a limited bag. Where are you getting these pictures?" I knew then I had to meet this woman. So, during the next cheer competition, I went over and spoke to her. We realized we were neighbors and the rest is history. I now have a Praying Friend, a Smart Friend, and yes, a rich friend! My kids love their house and have even taken rides in their helicopter! I'm not telling the story to brag, but to say, if you change your circle, you change your life. Of course, she is more than material value to me! That's just the bonus. But, if I didn't change my circle, I would have never met Cleo Oliver, who makes me smile every time we speak and makes me feel good as a person!

Now, you know that I am NOT going to let you get away from this chapter without doing some reflection. The people who you share time, energy, and space around are of too much importance. I wrote this part of the book with every fiber in my body. Like TLC said in their hit song, "What About Your Friends?"

1. List the names of the five people who you spend the most time with.

_____

_____

_____

_____

_____

_____

_____

_____

_____

_____

_____

_____

_____

_____

_____

2. Do your friends make you feel good?

_____

_____

_____

_____

_____

_____

_____

_____

_____

_____

_____

_____

_____

_____

_____

_____

3. How do you believe people would categorize you and your friends? What would you be most known for?

_____

_____

_____

_____

_____

_____

_____

_____

_____

_____

_____

_____

_____

_____

4. What do you and your friends talk about the most?

_____

_____

_____

_____

_____

_____

_____

_____

_____

_____

_____

_____

_____

_____

_____

_____

5. How is your intellect stimulated by the people in your circle?

_____

_____

_____

_____

_____

_____

_____

_____

_____

_____

_____

_____

_____

_____

_____

6. What do you like most about the people in your circle?

_____

_____

_____

_____

_____

_____

_____

_____

_____

_____

_____

_____

_____

_____

7. What do you like least about the people in your circle?

_____

_____

_____

_____

_____

_____

_____

_____

_____

_____

_____

_____

_____

_____

_____

_____

_____

8. What are your innermost thoughts after engaging in time with your friends?

_____

_____

_____

_____

_____

_____

_____

_____

_____

_____

_____

_____

_____

_____

Now that you've reflected deeply about the people who are in your inner circle, I want you to ask yourself if you are better for being around those people. Do they bring out the best in you? Do they push you to realize your greatest potential? Do you aspire to be better when you are in their presence? Do they accept you for who you are?

If you answered, "No" to any of those questions, you may need to address the role they serve in your life. You have to recognize that the people in our lives either take up space or fill it in. Remember, you have the power to decide who gets an invitation to use your time and your energy. When someone's season has passed, let them go, especially if they contribute to the downward spiral of your mental well-being. Sometimes in life, you will find that you have to be willing to LET SOME PEOPLE GO! If it means your sanity, then I say, DO IT! You must remember to look out for yourself so that you can be a blessing to someone else. The last thing that I will say here is, consider who your attention rises and decreases around. If you still haven't figured out how to determine who you should keep around versus who should go, add that to your laundry list of strategies. Either way, you deserve the absolute best from those around you. Make sure that you demand it.

*"Letting go of what used to be, also means having unspeakable faith for what will be."*

Chanita Foster

# Chapter 9: Lose Control, Gain Control

THERE IS A SONG by Fantasia, and before you even say anything, I know that I reference a lot of songs, but trust me, music is life. There are so many elements within the melodies, and the words prove to be powerful, or relatable, at different moments in our lives. The point that I am making is that the song by Fantasia is called, "Lose to Win." In the song, she speaks about being with a man who doesn't show reciprocity. He was deadweight, but out of habit and thoughts of necessity, she felt that she needed him. The power in the song evolves when she recognizes that to gain her sanctity and the ability to live abundantly, she must CUT THE DEADWEIGHT. Her happiness comes at the cost of losing him. She understands that she has to lose at love, to ever discover it again.

I reference this song, not because I am speaking about love, but because there is a powerful message in it. The concept of losing to gain is poignant for so many reasons. We must first be willing to recognize that we are not in control of every factor of our lives. Social media, and the new trends and messages of "Taking life by the horns" are great, and don't get me wrong, I don't believe for one minute that we should sit around and let life just happen, it is our responsibility to be actively involved in what we want to have happen and the pursuit of our dreams, but that being said, we must understand deeply that we don't have control of everything. Depression sneaks in, like a thief in the night, especially for those who feel out of control. The sad part is that if we took the time to recognize that there are some factors and moments that we can't control, we gain the freedom to make the best decisions in those moments. LOSING the notion that we can control every factor of our lives, is an attempt to WIN and is the perfect example of losing control to gain control.

I've mentioned this earlier, but I'd be doing you a disservice if I didn't say it again. There are so many times in our lives when we ATTEMPT to hold onto things that we cannot control. This can come in the form of people, places and things. You should probably go back and read that line again. I say, ATTEMPT, because if we were truly honest with ourselves, we would realize that we are not truly able to hold onto people, places, or things. The ability to do so is not in our control, and when we walk around believing that it is, we are not in touch with reality. This is why it hurts so bad when people exit our lives. If we operated under the auspices that we don't have the power to decide if someone stays or goes, we are empowered. It is a burden to carry the belief that can truly make people stay. During my depression, I had to learn that worrying about who would be in my life, was the least of my concerns. The people who wanted to be there, would be. It's as simple as that. Letting go of my grasp was the same as letting go of control. The more I let go, the less I felt the need to hold on. Have you ever experienced life with just the people who want to be there? IT IS A BREATH OF FRESH AIR! You haven't lived until you alleviate the pressure of who is in your life and who is not. Trust me, you will thank me later.

The control that I speak of is not limited to people, but can encompass places and things. I've already told you about the materialistic overhaul and how that can affect your overall state, but I do think it's important to point out that there are places that no longer serve you either. It is important for us to take a long look at the places that we frequent. It could be a bar, or it could be a church. It could be a friend's house, or it could be a family member's house. The bottom line is that it is enlightening to look at where you go and how those places make you feel. All of this matters. If you go places on a regular basis that don't make you feel good about you, STOP. I don't care where it is or who is there. If it makes you question your self-worth and does not contribute to the betterment of you, or ho you want to become, LET IT GO. This is another example of losing control to gain control. Trust me, I'm going somewhere with all of this. I'm going to give this to you another way. I want you to have as many examples as I can think of, because this factor alone can take you all the way out.

I remember, like it was yesterday. I got a phone call from the girl braiding my daughter's hair. She said, "Did you send someone to the house?"

"No," I replied. "I'm all the way in South Africa, why?"

"Someone just tried to open the front door and it was a guy!"

Now, let me paint the picture for you. My house is like Union Station. People are coming and going all the time. I love people, so everyday someone is stopping by to say hello, do business, leave kids (because we are like a daycare), or to eat food. So, my mind wasn't thinking anything negative at all. I told her to go look at the video monitor in the house. We have a monitor on the counter, showing all of the doors and windows, so don't come trying to break in. Lol

She looked at the monitor and said, "It's a tall man with a hood on!"

I was still calm and asked "Have you seen him before?"

"No," she stated. I told her to ask Jersey, aka Boss Hog, my daughter, to look at the monitor to see if she knew him.

Boss said, "No," and then screamed into the phone, "He's opening the basement door and coming in!"

"Hang up and call the police!" I then began calling friends and neighbors to go to my home immediately! It wasn't until I received a text that my heart dropped.

It read, "I am locked in the bathroom with Boss Hog and we are scared!"

As the tears flowed, I told her that they were lucky because on the top cabinet there was a hidden gun. (Yes, I have guns! Lots of them! Hidden all over the house! I'm from Detroit! Land of the Free and Home of the Brave! We have the right to bear arms and I exercise it for this very reason!) But that day we had a problem. The girl protecting my daughter exclaimed, "I can't shoot a gun!"

OK, pause the story. I know I'm off track, but ladies, especially if you are a single mother, PLEASE take a self-defense class and learn how to shoot a gun! It's a cold world we live in and it is your job to protect yourself and your children. Shout out to my dad, aka Billy Dent, for putting a gun in my hand and teaching me how to shoot during our trips to Northern Michigan. OK, back to the story.

She wouldn't get the gun. I'm in South Africa and they are in Atlanta, Georgia. It was out of my control. So, I kept calling people. Shout out to Pamela Endsley, who totaled her car in a car accident trying to get to Boss Hog that day!!! She ended up in the hospital trying to save my child and I am forever grateful. So, how did it end! I got the phone call that the police arrived, along with all the people I called, but the man had already run out of the house. No, they never caught him. With the incident over, I call Stormy Wellington, my friend, coach, and business partner, and she offered her Buckhead condo to my children, so they could get away and process it all. I have some amazing people in my life.

Once all was well at home, I walked into a room and presented the Total Life Changes opportunity to about a hundred people. I was late to the meeting because I was trying to handle all that had occurred in Atlanta from Africa. At the end, a woman raised her hand and said, "They came in and said you were late because someone was breaking into your house and your daughter was inside!"

"Yes, that is true!" I replied.

"Why aren't you upset or going crazy?"

And with that question I knew that I had fully mastered the ability to lose control to gain control. I responded "I have learned NOT to allow things I can't control, to run my life!"

Was I scared? Absolutely! My youngest of six children was in danger. Once all was clear, what could I do? Could I change the fact that he came into the house? Should I cry about it? Boss Hog was now safe. Should I do like most, pack up my things and go back to America? For what? It was late in the evening! Delta wasn't flying. So why cry all night about something I had no control over. Should I get on a plane and fly seventeen hours just to walk in my house and hug Boss? Hell No! That would be me allowing a situation I can't control, to control me! Want to stop being depressed? Stop allowing things you have no control over, to run your life! If I have no control, I move on. This is the area that is hardest for most!

Here is the blatant reality. Most of the things that we worry about are NOT IN OUR CONTROL to begin with. Truly grasping this concept, made me look at myself and what I was capable of in a much different way. We spend so much time worrying about what will be, that we miss out on truly enjoying what is.

The need to control actually limits us much more than we could ever imagine. I also learned that being the master of control also makes you less fun. Have you ever been around someone at an event that is supposed to be fun, but they want to plan everything? It takes away from enjoying the elements of surprise. Control freaks are probably the unhappiest group of people. I would know because I have been one. The truth is they aren't having fun, nor are the people around them. The need to control, in my opinion, is an empty promise. I had to sit back and ask myself, what was better about having controlled the situation? I couldn't ever really seem to come up with anything. This is how I knew that I had to let that type of behavior go, in order to live my best life and gain access to true happiness.

I'm not saying that this is true for everyone, but I do think that being controlling can open doors for depression as well. Demanding control leaves you more susceptible to being let down and disappointed. I now believe that when we desire control, we must also examine what it is about us that feels the need to take command? Are we controlling to ensure the safety of our children? Are we controlling because we don't trust our spouse to do something the way that we would do it? Are we controlling because we feel out of control? There are so many factors to consider. Even so, what I do know is that we cannot rise if we are weighed down with the bricks of control.

I knew that I wasn't making this up, when I stumbled across what is referred to as the Law of Surrender. Even in large corporations, who teach leadership and train their top-level executives, they discuss the power in managing employees rather than micromanaging. It is a common practice to act in accordance with the notion that typically, employees want to perform well. What if we applied this same concept in our own lives? What if we believed that everyone, including ourselves, wanted to perform well at life? The problem is that we set the expectations of how the people in our lives should behave, where they should be, and what they should be doing. Can you believe that we even have expectations for how they should make us feel? It sounds ridiculous when you read it, but we do it every day. I still do.

The bottom line is that we have no control over any of this. The bottom line is that until we recognize just how little power we have, we will always be disappointed. The bottom line is that if we don't let go, we could lose our sanity. The bottom line is that the only person whose actions we can control is our own. I think I nailed that. You have to be willing to lose control to gain control. Now go tell somebody! We all need a dose of this reality.

*"You're allowed to cry, but never allowed to give up."*

Chanita Foster

# Chapter 10: 15 Minutes to Cry, Then Get Gangsta

AS WOMEN WE CRY! I don't care how tough you are as a woman, at some point you have a break down and you cry. When I was depressed, there was a lot, and I mean a lot of crying going on. I remember that people would call and I would just be crying. One of my best guy friends, Jevon Sims, would call and I would just cry on the phone. He would say "Chanita, what's wrong?"

My reply was always the same, "I don't know!" Can you imagine what was going through his mind as a friend? He didn't stop calling though and what's more, he never stopped asking. Most people just thought I was tripping, that I should have been able to finish the sentence, answer their question. But I wasn't trippin', I was DEPRESSED.

It's crucial for me to point out to you any and all strategies that helped me to get through. When I was coming out of the depressions, an invaluable lesson that I learned was that it was OK to cry. Sometimes people equate crying with weakness. I believe that to be the contrary. Crying can be cleansing in many ways. We need to allow ourselves to acknowledge any hurt, discomfort, pain, or anxiety that we may be feeling. Sweeping those feelings under the rug is what takes us to places that we had never dreamed of, or wanted to go. Depression is not a destination that I wish upon anyone.

I think that we should not only feel entitled to our crying moments, but that we should also work to welcome them. I do, however, feel that crying should serve a purpose. I know that you might think that I'm crazy for telling you to cry with a purpose, but I mean it. If you spend your days crying and nothing happens as a result, it is time that is wasted. If the cry can cleanse, or heal, or even just validate your feelings, then it becomes worth it. The storm doesn't have to last forever. As they would say in church, "Joy comes in the morning." Knowing how to recognize that morning time is just as critical as the cry itself. This is the difference between someone who cries and has yet to figure out why they are crying, and those who recognize the power in the crying process.

Like I said, it's OK to cry, but do it with purpose — cry for fifteen minutes and then get Gangsta! Why do I say that? Because crying can emotionally and mentally bring you all the way down, if you let it. Have you ever cried so much that when you were done you needed a nap? Now, imagine doing that every day! How can you be effective? It's impossible. So, you have to recognize the cry and what is making you cry.

I am reminded of a story that was told to me that further explains my point. Pay ATTENTION, I'M GOING IN!

There was a little girl named Amber, who based on outward appearances, had an amazing life. She was raised in a single parent home with her father, but he never missed a beat. From a very young age, he would take her to the salon to get her hair done and the nail shops to get her nails done. From the outside looking in, she appeared to have it all. Her father was there to pick her up every day from school and he attended every school event that he could. He even managed to serve on the PTA, and the moms all loved him. He was one of the few dads who actually participated. Amber was well known and well liked. People always wondered where her mother was, but often hesitated to ask the question, as it could make Amber uncomfortable. The father did such an amazing job with Amber, that it seemed adults even hesitated to ask the father about the whereabouts of the mother. Through elementary school, Amber and her father were inseparable. Amber was always extremely pleasant and outgoing. She went on to achieve academically and was of course, the apple of her father's eye. After making countless academic gains, Amber was accepted to a school for students who were advanced. The school boasted an International Baccalaureate program. That is a program for students who excel academically, above the standard advanced curriculum. The IB Program would ensure that Amber was set on the right path for college and her father wanted nothing more. Attending this school would mean that Amber would have to commute with her father to another side of town, versus attending the high school that she was zoned for. It was said that Amber told her father that she didn't want to attend the school, but she could never give her father a specific reason as to why. Up until that point, she had never backed down from a challenge. As any good father would, Amber's father pushed her to attend the school. He wanted what was best for her, and he wasn't about to stop acting in her best interest. He figured that since she was a teenager, she was less excited about academic challenges and more excited about the opportunities to be social. That's what teenagers do right? In Amber's case, WRONG.

When Amber began attending the high school, everything about her demeanor changed. Her teachers reported to her father that she appeared to be very distant. She seldom smiled, and the social butterfly they had been introduced to, seemed to have vanished. Amber began to withdraw socially and wanted less and less to be around people her own age. Her father even noticed that she would reject invitations extended to her by other students. He couldn't quite place what was manifesting in Amber's life. Her father assumed that Amber was being a normal teenager.

Although she continued to make good grades, her father noticed that she became very standoffish, even at home. When he would ask her if there was anything going on, she would always reply, "I'm fine, Dad". In a desperate attempt to find the little girl that he had raised, he asked Amber if she would be willing to attend a counseling session. He figured that if she would not speak to him, maybe she would speak to someone who was neutral.

Amber agreed, begrudgingly. As they approached the office, her father stopped her and said, "Amber, if there is anything that you can do today, in this office, that you cannot do at home, just do it. I just want to get my little girl back."

Amber entered the counseling room and closed the door behind her. Her father stayed in the foyer of the office and began to pace. He was so concerned that he would lose his daughter forever. After about an hour, her father heard the handle on the door turn and Amber emerged. The doctor asked Amber to sit outside while she had a moment with her father. Amber followed the doctor's directive and took a seat in the foyer.

When the father sat down in the office, he was anxious to discuss the findings. "Mr. Bastian, I think we have discovered a missing piece to your puzzle."

"Please, tell me. Is there something that I can do? How can I help her?"

"I believe that it is more simple than complicated," she explained.

"Thank God. Please, what did she do while in here with you?"

"Well, for about thirty of the sixty minutes that she was here, she sat and just cried."

"Cried? I'm afraid that I don't know what you mean."

"I know that it sounds complicated, Mr. Bastian, but please trust me, it's really not. I allowed her to cry without interruption and afterwards, we discussed why she cried."

With a look of intense bewilderment, her father asked, "Well, what did she say?"

"Well, Mr. Bastian, I'm afraid that Amber will have to tell you that. It is imperative that tonight, the two of you sit together and discuss today's session. Trust me, she will give you an answer that is far better than anything that I could ever say. I'm certain that it will clear up a great deal of uncertainty for her and for you. I would really like to see her back again this week. Can you promise to bring her to the office for another appointment?"

Dazed and confused, Mr. Bastian said, "Yes. Yes, I'm sure that I can. Thank you, Doctor. We will see you again this week." Mr. Bastian exited the doctor's office, paid his co pay, and escorted Amber out to the car. On the way home, they picked up food and then rode the rest of the way amidst silence and the jazz music that he always played in the car.

When they arrived home, Amber grabbed her things and Mr. Bastian sat in the car, overwhelmed from the day. He wondered what could have been bothering his baby girl so deeply that she couldn't tell him. He didn't want to pressure her, but he needed to know. As he walked into their home, he called for her, "Amber, come downstairs, Honey. We need to talk."

"Coming," she replied.

"Here, sit down next to me. Come on over to your papa." She smiled and for the first time in a long time, he saw the resemblance of the little girl who he had raised with his whole heart. "Now, tell me. What happened in the office today? Why did the doctor say that you would be better after today's visit? What did you do while in there?"

"You want the real truth, Dad?" she asked.

"Yes, of course."

"Well, the doctor told me that there had to be something that I was holding in. She said she sensed that there was something that I was holding onto and that I needed to let it go. In that moment, when she told me that it was safe to let it go, I began to cry profusely. The tears were streaming down my eyes and I couldn't seem to get it under control." By this time, Mr. Bastian was crying. As Amber spoke, she began to cry too. "Do you remember when you asked me why I didn't want to go to that school?"

"Of course, but I still don't understand."

"Well, when Mom died, I remember riding home in the limousine from her funeral. The whole time, I had my head buried in the seat. The first time I looked out of the window from the limousine, I saw that high school. I'm not sure why I saw it, but I did. When we got home, I found a letter next to the side of my bed that Mom had written to me before she died, and it said, 'Don't cry for me. Be strong for Daddy.' I never knew until this day, that she didn't mean that I couldn't cry at all. From the time that I read that letter, I promised myself that I would never cry because you already had so much to deal with, trying to raise me alone. Today, in that office, when the doctor told me to that I could let go of what I was holding onto, that was it. The high school had reminded me of Mom's death. Just being there, made me so sad.

By this time, you can image the tears that Mr. Bastian was producing. That night, both Amber and her father sat and cried in each other's arms. For the first time, they both cried to cleanse, to heal, and to acknowledge their pain.

Amber went on to graduate from that same high school because she realized that more than anything, her mother wanted her to get the best education possible. On her graduation day, she held her diploma towards the sky, to dedicate her education and journey to her mother. Needless to say, Mr. Bastian was proud.

Together, they had learned a valuable lesson about the power of crying. They also demonstrated through their actions what it meant to get gangsta after a good cry. My point is that we all deserve to cleanse and cry. Doing so gives us a fighting chance at being real with the person in the mirror and not shoving our feelings to the side.

YAHOO! That story gets me every time! I'm sure it almost took you out too. It's touching, but it's also a testament. So, while I don't hold myself back from crying, my crying is now different. I ask myself, "Chanita why are you crying? Are you hurt? Is it worth crying about?" Yes, I talk myself through crying. (I know you are saying, "This girl is always talking to herself," but yes, it works! Lol.) I limit my crying so it doesn't consume me! No more crying about the same thing for days. No more hindering my day to day due to tears. Even when I need a good cry, I put on my cry song! Are you asking, "What's a cry song?" Chile, a cry song is that song that you are guaranteed to hear and start crying! Don't act like you don't know! For most of us, it's that church song that sends us into tears! As soon as it plays, you just start crying. It may also be that old school R&B song from your first love or hard break up. The one that you know every word to! What I'm getting at is, play one of those songs and cry it out! Sing the lyrics. Let snot run down your nose and face. Scream! But, once the song is over, you wipe those tears, clean up that snot, and freshen your face because it's time for you to get gangster!

A cry party is usually two songs, back to back, so you can get your full fifteen minutes of crying! Now, here's the hard part. When it's over, don't cry about it again! I know it's difficult, but why keep crying about the same thing over and over again? Do tears really solve why you feel the way you feel? Stop crying about it. Stop giving it your time, energy, and emotion! You want to get out of a depression and stay out of it? Stop crying about the same thing, and find something that can empower you instead. This is key, so I'll repeat it. STOP CRYING AND FIND SOMETHING THAT CAN EMPOWER YOU INSTEAD! Trust me, I'm not telling you not to cry. I'm telling you to cry with purpose. Life is a fight and we take some tough hits. We MUST find routines and rituals to help us weather the storm. So, like I said, cry for fifteen minutes if you must, but your next move is your best move. Make it gangsta!

*"You can't expect to see results, if you're not willing to get your hands dirty."*

Chanita Foster

# Chapter 11: You Betta Work!

I MADE THE DECISION, long ago, to pour my heart out for you because I truly wanted to do everything in my power to make sure that you didn't have to hurt the way that I hurt. My life has been filled with blue skies and grey skies, nevertheless, I'm still standing. Today, I look back over my life and I bask in the fact that I was able to bend, but not break. Lord knows, there were so many times that I wanted to throw my hands up with it all, but that's not reality, nor is it what I am made of. Somewhere along the way, I forgot the power that has always been inside of me. Those moments of weakness could have been too much to bear, and for some, they proved to be just that, too much.

I serve a God, who created me with an abundance of resources, from which to replenish, rediscover, and channel all that I am and all that I am destined to become. The good news, is that even though I have overcome and I stand having triumphed, God is not through with me yet. I recognize that life may bring more hits. The difference for me today is that I am ready. I have allowed myself to put on the armor of help. That armor that I speak of is a robust list of strategies that I now know to reference when life hits. And as much as I tried to get away from referencing football, I am the top draft pick, with the ability to move, and cut, and pivot at a moment's noticed when life hits.

If you have gotten all the way to this point in the book, and you haven't been paying attention, this is the moment to do so. My greatest gift to you is all of the strategies that I have used to get me to today. These strategies saved my life and I know with certainty that they can help you to channel your power. We all have the same power to overcome, to fall forward, to take life by the horns, and to not become victims of our circumstances. We all have the power to triumph. Now, listen up, because this train is about to move real fast. We have a final destination that I'd like to call success! It awaits us all. Now get into these strategies.

## 1. Categorize Everything

It is possible that I took for granted that life could break me down. Perhaps I believed that I could handle whatever came my way. Perhaps many of us do and maybe that's the problem. We often don't believe that life can deliver hits that can take us out, and in turn we are ill prepared. We must learn to recognize which type of moments make us happy and which types take our happiness away. The simple ability to distinguish between the two is life changing. Recognize that life has the power to happen and it has the capacity to make or break you. I had to find what my happy was to breakthrough.

## 2. Consider the Small Things

Who knew that small things could trigger unhappiness? I sure didn't. We always hear people say, "Don't sweat the small stuff." Some even refer to the insignificant moments as "petty," and while I too believe that many things are not worth our time, or energy, I do believe that we need to know what small things are non-negotiable for us.

There is a quote that speaks about the significance of small things. The quote references that if you think you are too small to be significant, consider the impact of the mosquito. We all know what that means, so I know I don't have to go any further. My point is that small things can be triggers too. Being aware of them, puts us ahead of the game. Furthermore, we can learn to truly not sweat the small stuff, when we know what can take us all the way out. That's real talk! I hope you got that! You'd be surprised. I learned that if my kids take food off my plate, it makes me unhappy. It is not that I don't want to share with my kids; I am always willing to give them the last and the best of what I have. What I learned to recognize was that because I am always in a state of giving, sitting down to eat is a moment that I need to take for myself. My children taking food from my plate, made me feel like that moment and that right was violated. Now, that's a candid example of a small thing if I've ever heard one. But hey, I said I would keep it real with you and that's exactly what I'm doing here. Stay with me.

## 3. Meet & Greet Resentment.

I felt a lot of resentment regarding the NFL wives stuff. That part of my life was over, and I truly didn't like the way that it being over made me feel. In retrospect, I think it was more about the way that others valued the superficiality of the sport. I have since accepted that I had different values than many of those whom I had accepted as counterparts. It was far more important to me that my family demonstrated love and an understanding of why we needed to do our parts to make the world a better place, than discussing what team my husband used to, or no longer played for. That rude awakening caused me to resent that part of my life. To heal, my goal became to point out, specifically, the stuff that made me angry and to (THIS IS BIG) find a way to LET IT GO. YES! LET IT GO! How would harboring resentment for people, who didn't even have my best interest in mind, help me? How could that act make a difference in my journey? It only served to further agitate my depression. Letting go of the feelings of resentment changed my life, and it can do the same for you. Consider this: If you have a job and get fired from it, how can you go to lunch with those same people? When life changes, we must be clear on how we need to change to accommodate it.

## 4. Get Rid of People

Anything that is toxic must go and that includes people. I have said it before, and I will say it again. People have seasons in our lives. When the season ends, we must learn to clean the slate. This is not to say that we have to end relationships, but we must end the way in which we expose ourselves to anything that compromises our mental disposition. When battling depression, or living life in general, the company that you keep will prove to be a huge factor in determining your emotional well-being. I must also be clear that there are no limits here. We have to find the strength to become human filters for our spirits. If there are any signs of anything other than someone who has our overall well-being in mind, they must be alleviated. This can include family members, friends, associates, co-workers, and everything in between. I've even taken the liberty of giving you three specific examples of folks that you can do yourself a favor and get rid of.

### The Critics

If you encounter someone who is more critical of you than supportive, chances are your time and energy around them should be limited. It will not contribute in a positive way to your overall self-perception. This is not to say that everyone needs to be in the "yes" choir, but those who truly want to see you win should have just as much praise as criticism.

### Time Thieves

Have you ever been around someone and afterwards felt like you wasted the time you spent with them? This is huge. Time is the only resource that you can't get back and can't make more of. That said, if you are not better, happier, richer, closer to God, or inspired after your time with someone, you might be wasting a resource that is too great to lose.

### The Careless

Chile, if you encounter someone who hasn't a care in the world, chances are you are one of the things that they don't care about. Now don't get this confused with living a carefree life. That is not who I am talking about. I am speaking about folks who are too self-absorbed to notice if you are hurting. If the people that you spend time with can't demonstrate a genuine concern for you, you might need to reconsider how much time or energy you give to them. Another example of this is people who use all of your time together to talk about their own concerns, with little regard for yours. Plain and simple, you deserve better.

## 5. Take Moments of Solitude

As I began to find the value in spending moments alone, I began to study more in the Bible. I recognized patterns that I hadn't recognized before. Whenever God was getting ready to send people on a mission or journey, many of them went into solitude. It was also revealed to me that when you are depressed, you are already in solitude. The fact of the matter is that you must go deeper in an attempt to get to know yourself. You must be able to answer questions that only you can answer. Who are you? Where are you along your journey of life? Where do you want to be? Being in solitude allows you to take a realistic look at all of those questions and to truly analyze the next steps that can position you for what you want to manifest in your life.

## 6. Own It

Until you deplete all of your victim ideologies, you will never truly heal. No matter what has happened in your life, there was some role that you played in it. Just as the hero had a role, every person does. I won what has not gone well in my life. I am not looking for sympathy, or excuses, or someone to tell me that it was "not my fault." I ask myself questions like:

1. What part did I play in what triggered my depression?
2. Was I a bad mother? Friend? Wife?

The hardest thing to do is to look in the mirror and tell your truth. In moments of complete honesty and transparency, I realized that I was not always a good person to other people. I was very aggressive and very opinionated. I even own the fact that some of the situations that I found myself in, I created.

I believe that it is second nature for us to place blame on others. This is not to say that we are to blame for what has happened to us, but like I said, we have a role. We want to place the blame when friendships fall apart, but we played a part in the gossip. We want to place blame when relationships fail, but we played a part in the messiness. We want to defend when others speak out against us, but we played the part in trying to defend situations that had nothing to do with us.

## 7. Make a Change

A major development for me was recognizing that I needed to change. Far too often, I took on battles that really were not mine.

Whether it was something going on with someone else that I believed that I had to help them through, or finding a way to accept personal criticism, positive or negative.

There were so many things that I learned about myself during the process of healing. There were so many massive lessons that I gleaned. One in particular was that every fight was not my fight. I now bask in the fact that everything does not involve me, or require my energy. I now recognize that every fight for justice is not my cross to bear.

This is a simple, yet profound concept, but believe me when I say, owning your role in what happens in your life, makes you far more powerful than you will ever know. TRY IT! YOU CAN THANK ME LATER!

## 8. Unfollow in Real Life

Here's a big thing. I believe that social media can drive people into a depression. No one is going to post that their lights got cut off. No one is going to post that their kid got a bad note from school. No one is going to post that their husband is cheating. Social media has taught us to give the best, but THAT AIN'T REALISTIC! Life is not flowers and rainbows every day of the week. We all have real life struggles that are not played out on social media. I had to recognize that social media was teaching us all to engage in unnecessary comparisons that wreaked havoc on our self-esteem, self-perception, and thus our perceived value for what was happening in our own lives.

The best strategy that I developed to combat this was to unfollow some folks. I even developed a set of criteria from which to unfollow. You want to know it, right? You should. You need this, trust me.

If they were not inspiring me, taking me to a place that I wanted to go, helping me to see a new perspective, or keeping me spiritually grounded, I unfollowed them. You have to ask yourself, who are you following? What can this person do for your life, besides show you gossip or fashion?

I began to hit the follow button to engage with philanthropists, nonprofits, pastors, and those who inspired me. I realized that I was following a bunch of superficial people who only placed value on material things. There were times that I would log in and see my old life, or people talking about red carpet events, and I had to ask myself: "How is that making me feel?" Well, it didn't feel good to me. Now, when I scroll through, I see Shery Riley, Danny Johnson, Tammy Franklin, Tonya Baker, Marvin Sapp, and the like. I see people that inspire and uplift me. Today, my social media pushes me to be better because I am following people whom I either admire or respect for their contributions to the world. As I always say, "What you feed your mind, body, and soul, are sure to be reflected in the fruits that you bear."

## 9. Richer, Smarter, Closer to God

You will hear me reference Coach Stormy Wellington often because she is just that amazing. She once said, "If it doesn't make me richer, smarter, or bring me closer to God, then I don't need it in my life." Now that's real talk. During the process of moving out of my depression, I would talk to myself on several occasions. The interrogation was serious. I would continually say, "OK, Chanita, is this person going to make you richer, smarter, or bring you closer to God?" If my answer was "no," I knew that they weren't for me. There is not a lot to be said here. The bottom line is that every person who takes up space in your life and in your heart, should enhance who you are in some way. By the same token, you should also do the same for them. Richer, smarter, or closer to God is a great measuring stick in my book, literally!

## 10. Accountability Partner

Ravon Robinson, Ebony Electra, Sabrina Patterson, and Deidra Ellington. These are the names of some very significant people in my life. Over the years, they have evolved into what I refer to as my accountability partners. Their roles in my life are at times unexplainable. We all can benefit from accountability partners during our lives, not just before, during, or after a depression. However, to rise from the darkness of depression, they are key.

Whenever I felt like I was going to slip back into a dark hole, I could call any one of those four people, and they would hold me accountable for who I was and for reaching my potential in absence of depression.

At any given time, I could call them and know that our conversations wouldn't turn into gossip sessions, but therapy sessions. They knew to keep it real and how to keep me present: "Tell me what we can do to fix this. Tell me what we can do to turn the corner."

Truth be told, depression is often hardest for those closest to you because they don't understand what you are going through. Those four women knew that overcoming depression was a journey and knew that I was a work in progress. We all need someone that can be accountable on the bad days, that can pray with you, talk to you, serve as a solution finder, and someone that won't allow you to have a pity party. Sometimes, we just want to talk, and need someone to listen. There were times that I just needed a set of ears, not necessarily someone who was trying to fix anything. Outside of professional help, accountability partners can prove to be allies in the fight. I can honestly say that I am better for having had them in my corner.

## 11. Seek Professional Help

Taking the step to get professional help is a huge one. If you discover your strength to do this, you will also discover that you have just managed to lay a heavy burden down. Getting professional help is considered taboo, especially within some cultures, but that should be the least of your concerns, if you really want to get to the root of what is going on with you. Fortunately, there is no shortage of help. There is a wealth of information that can assist you in finding the right professional to work with. There is so much danger in trying to weather the storm of depression alone. Far too often, it turns into a bigger issue. What am I saying? YOU NEED PROFESSIONAL HELP. One of the only ways to get out of this rut, is to have someone to speak with and help you to identify the triggers, and strategies to overcome your depression. The truth is that when you dig deep, a lot of pain and root causes arise, but you don't have to go it alone.

## 12. Finding Your "Why"

Trying to understand why you exist, is a journey that never ends. I now recognize that the point of living life is to remain in a constant state of discovery. We learn new things about ourselves and the way in which we perceive happiness almost daily. It is my belief that our definition of what makes us happy is ever changing, as is, how we gift the world with what we have. Our happiness is deeply rooted in our existence. That being said, the first step is recognizing that we DO have something of value to offer the world. After we discover what we have to offer, we must never forget it. Although discovering that "something" is not easy, many have managed to stumble upon it. I call it the "WHY." Even if you've managed to discover it, it is possible that along the journey of life, you have forgotten it, as many of us do. I had forgotten mine and it contributed to the spiral of depression that manifested in my life. As women, we get wrapped up in our roles in life. I would even venture to say that we begin to believe that our "why" is embedded in caring for our husbands and/or our children. It is not. Neither our jobs, nor our community work is the reason why we exist. If you believe that you only wake up every day to serve your kids, community, job, or whatever else, I urge you to dig a little deeper into the desires of your soul. I personally believe that nothing could be farther from the truth. I think that you deserve to ask yourself, unapologetically: What is your "Why"? What fills you? What are you passionate about? What do you dream about? What will you still be passionate about if you were alone in the world? Trust me, discovering these answers will change your perspective on a lot of things. Of course, we are here to make the world a better place, but far too often we put too much emphasis there and we forget how to make ourselves happy. This is another entry point for depression.

For me, I remember a time that I thought my "why" was rooted in my philanthropy. There came a time when financially, I was not able to support others the way that I wanted to. When you go from giving thousands of dollars per month, to much less, it affects you. It took a toll on me. Serving people made me happy, and when I couldn't do it any longer, in that way, I lost my "why." The moment you lose your "why," is the day that you don't want to wake up anymore. It is the day that it suddenly gets hard to get out of bed.

HEAR THIS CLEARLY. Your "why" has everything to do with you, and no one else. You exist for so many reasons, but to discover what makes you happy must become a top priority. This is the only way that you can be whole enough to truly give to others. If you keep pouring from an empty glass, you will eventually run out of water. You have a responsibility to discover, and hold onto your "why" at all costs.

WHEN YOU LOSE YOUR "WHY," YOU LOSE YOUR WAY!

## 13. Celebrate the Small Stuff

Let me tell you something: life is hard. We expect so much of ourselves and I truly believe that we fall short when praising ourselves. The world has taught us to stop praising small feats and only recognize monumental goals. This is the dumbest thing that I have ever heard. No large goal can be accomplished, in the absence of the small goals that assist you in getting across the finish line.

Amidst depression, I learned that if I didn't allow myself to celebrate the small stuff, I would have really gone off the deep end. Hell, if I went one day without cussing, I had to create a celebration for that. If I had a weight loss goal or a work-related goal and I accomplished it, I would celebrate that. If I had a nonprofit goal and I met it, I celebrated it. I stopped waiting for the big things. A lot of us are waiting for the big promotion, the big marriage, the big birthday, but we are missing all of the amazing life that happens along the way. If you begin to celebrate the small things, you can more easily accept happiness into your life.

Prior to recognizing the importance of the small celebrations, I felt like I was failing because I didn't have the next big thing. If I wasn't winning an award or huge accolade, I felt like I was failing. ALL LIES! News flash: the next big thing was that you were blessed to wake up this morning and see your kids off to school, in good health. Those things that we take for granted are the next big thing.

## 14. Affirmations

Along my journey towards healing, I began to look around the world at people who I deemed to be successful. A common thread that I found amongst them was the power of affirmations. It seemed that those who were successful, and leading healthy flourishing lives, seamlessly included affirmations within their day to day activities.

My friend and business partner, Coach Stormy Wellington, taught me affirmations. I never even knew what an affirmation was before I met her. Affirmations are when we speak positive thoughts into our lives. She spoke affirmations and I realized that they were an untapped source of power for when I felt weak. I began to recognize the power in encouraging and inspiring myself. A lot of people want a magic wand to change their lives, or to take them to the peak of success, but what I've learned is that the journey of life is just that — a journey. Along the journey, we are responsible for our happiness. YOU ARE THE ONLY PERSON WHO CAN BE RESPONSIBLE FOR YOUR HAPPINESS! You are the only person who can be responsible for attracting the things that you want in your life. It's yours.

I began to recite exactly what I wanted. Here are some of the affirmations I would say:

- I'm a money magnet.
- Everybody that I come into contact with will become a resource for me to accomplish my goals.

- It is my season.
- I am a champion.
- No weapon formed against me shall prosper.
- I am the head and not the tail.
- I will hear the voice of the Holy Spirit within.

The last one listed is my personal favorite. I now even use my affirmations as my hashtags on my social media platforms. I want to be surrounded by those words that claim victory in my life. I often place them in my car, and on the bathroom mirror. To overcome depression or any dark moment, you have to remain fixated on positive patterns of thought. Affirmations are priceless and today, I consider them to be an integral part of my life.

# Conclusion

LIKE THE SONG SAYS, "If you don't know me by now, you will never never never never know me." When I tell you that I have left it all on the stage, like Patti Labelle leaves her eyelashes and heels after she performs, I have left it all in this book for you, and THIS IS NOT EVENT MY MEMOIR! Trust and believe, you will get that book one day too. This purpose of this book was to give you a transparent look into depression, and the ways it creeps — like a thief in the night — into the deepest moments of your inner being. More importantly, these pages are filled with ways to get in front of the problem. I don't want anyone to ever feel that their feelings are not valid. No matter how big or how small something may be, we must be empowered to call that "thing" by name and determine if it should be allowed to take up time, space, and energy in our lives. We DESERVE BETTER. Depression is not who we are. Depression was not who I was, but it was something that happened to me. As I have mentioned, life happens to all of us. Knowing what to do when it happens, is the key.

I made the determination that I would be fully transparent because I now recognize the power in doing so. Some may feel that the subject is taboo, but I couldn't care less! I will continue to scream from the mountaintops about my personal experiences, to ensure that everyone who is willing to listen, and even those who may feel that they don't need to hear this message, can recognize the signs and gain access to some strategies to heal, or to know when to seek the help that is needed to overcome.

I am not a victim, nor was I ever. I am not easily broken, nor was I ever. I am not weak, nor was I ever. I am a woman, full of heart, strength, valor, might, and I am determined to see those around me win. I recognize my power and all of my capabilities, and it is my intent to walk fully in them. I also know that in order to perform at my highest level, I have to first be mentally healthy. I truly want you to take a long hard look at yourself and the people in your life, and determine what will make you happy. For some strange reason, I feel like many of us haven't learned what makes us happy. This is detrimental in so many ways, and it can contribute more than we could ever have imagined to us becoming depressed. The stories and strategies that I have shared with you are like armor before battle. Put them on. I did, and I am much better for having done so.

Today, any and everything that stands in the way of my mental health is blocked, unapologetically. I will not allow any circumstances to stand in the way of who I am destined to be, or my ability to help others realize their full potential. I wrote this book because I know that we all need a safe place to heal. If my messages of hope and love can save just one person, I will know that I have done what I set out to do.

# Do This for Me

ALL WISE TEACHING tells us to write the vision and make it plain. For many, this manifests in vision boards and vision board parties. I'm not knocking it, I just see no value in vision boards or vision board parties. What if you place a photo of a Range Rover on your board? What happens next? You look at it for the next year and it magically appears in your garage? That makes no sense, right? And, while I hate vision boards, and vision board parties, I do believe, that we should envision what we want to have happen in our lives. If you are going to write a vision, or create a vision board, I believe you must also create a plan of action to reach the goal. My question will always be, "How?"

Our thoughts become things. Instead of creating a vision board, I write my LIFE ROADMAP. I began to write the small goals that I needed to achieve, so I could reach the big goals. Most of the time when I talk to people and they say they want to make a million dollars, I ask how much they made last week? If they say $100, then why are we speaking about a million dollars? We need to celebrate and acknowledge the small goals along the way that can lead us to the well of the larger goal. Every large goal should be broken into digestible steps. Listen, I say, "Get you some cake and some balloons," when you reach a small goal on the road towards a big one. Promise me, that you will do this for me.

To take things a step further, I'm challenging you to write five small goals that you want to accomplish over the next year. These goals should be part of your larger, future goals. Believe me when I say, that everything you want, need, deserves, and desire is within your reach, if you remember that every vision, requires a plan of action.

1._____

_____

_____

2._____

_____

_____

3._____

_____

_____

4._____

_____

_____

5._____

_____

_____

# #CC
# Chanita's Challenge

I KNOW YOU THINK that I am always asking you to do something. I AM! I ask because I know that you haven't read this far, without needing to do what I am asking of you. Healing and overcoming takes work. You've got to be willing to do it, but trust me when I say that you are not alone. I'm challenging you to thirty Days of Affirmations that are purposed to create behavior that results in you learning how to pour into you. The greatest project that you will ever work on is you. I now know that more than ever. These affirmations that I have created are super simple and to the point. It is about you taking a small piece of the day for you. You deserve this more than you know. Let's work!

**Day 1** Today, I will listen to my feelings.
**Day 2** I will nourish myself.
**Day 3** I will bring positive energy into a room.
**Day 4** I have access to unlimited resources.
**Day 5** I will forgive others.
**Day 6** I will forgive myself.
**Day 7** I will proclaim that "All is Well."
**Day 8** I am open to change.
**Day 9** I will make the choice to feel good about myself.
**Day 10** I am worthy of love.
**Day 11** I will walk in purpose.

Day 12 Today, I honor who I am.

Day 13 I am worthy of my dreams.

Day 14 I will exercise gratitude today.

Day 15 I draw love from others.

Day 16 I am a magnet for miracles.

Day 17 I will bend, but I will not break.

Day 18 I am creating the life that I want.

Day 19 I can.

Day 20 I will witness and walk in abundance.

Day 21 I can accept change.

Day 22 I will give love to others.

Day 23 I am more than enough.

Day 24 All that I seek is within me.

Day 25 I am healed.

Day 26 Doors of opportunity will open for me.

Day 27 I am alive. It is well.

Day 28 I will speak loving words to myself.

Day 29 I claim my power.

Day 30 I can change my life.

# NOTES

## Preface

1. Laura A. Pratt, Ph.D, and Debra J. Brody, M.P.H. "Depression in the U.S. Household Population, 2009-2012," Centers for Disease Control and Prevention, December 3, 2014, Accessed October 25, 2017, https://www.cdc.gov/nchs/data/databriefs/db172.htm.

## Glossary

1. Merriam-Webster Medical Dictionary, "Depression," Merriam-Webster, Accessed October 25, 2017, https://www.merriam-webster.com/dictionary/depression#medicalDictionary.

2. Merriam-Webster Medical Dictionary, "Psychology," Merriam-Webster, Accessed October 25, 2017, https://www.merriam-webster.com/dictionary/psychology#medicalDictionary.

3. Merriam-Webster Medical Dictionary, "Psychiatry," Merriam-Webster, Accessed October 25, 2017, https://www.merriam-webster.com/dictionary/psychiatry#medicalDictionary.

4. Merriam-Webster Medical Dictionary, "Therapy," Merriam-Webster, Accessed October 25, 2017, https://www.merriam-webster.com/dictionary/therapy#medicalDictionary.

## Chapter 6 - Who Can I Run To

1. "Depression," Centers for Disease Control and Prevention, March 30, 2016, Accessed October 24, 2017, https://www.cdc.gov/mentalhealth/basics/mental-illness/depression.htm.

2. "Major Depression Among Adults," National Institute of Mental Health, Accessed October 24, 2017, https://www.nimh.nih.gov/health/statistics/prevalenc e/major-depression-among-adults.shtml.

3. "Depression," About Depression - Depression and Bipolar Support Alliance, Accessed October 24, 2017, http://www.dbsalliance.org/site/PageServer?pagename =education_depression.

4. "Depression: MedlinePlus," MedlinePlus Trusted Health Information for You, Accessed October 23, 2017, https://medlineplus.gov/depression.html.

5. "Depression," World Health Organization, Accessed October 24, 2017, http://www.who.int/mental_health/management/depr ession/en/.

6. Urban Dictionary, "Trippin," Urban Dictionary, Accessed October 24, 2017, https://www.urbandictionary.com/define.php?term=tr ippin.

## Chapter 7 - WHEN IT ALL FALLS DOWN

1. Urban Dictionary, "Trippin," Urban Dictionary, Accessed October 24, 2017, https://www.urbandictionary.com/define.php?term=tr ippin.

# About the Author

CHANITA FOSTER, Mompenuer, is the mother to Team Foster. Although Chanita's life has been successful, in 2014 she discovered she was suffering from depression. Through that journey of recovery, birthed her willingness to join the cast of BETHer reality show, *From The Bottom Up*. Although she swore off reality television, after previously starring on the VH1 Hit Series, *Football Wives*, Chanita believed returning to television would give her a platform to talk about depression.

As a serialpenuer, in 2015 Chanita Foster locked arms with millionaire Stormy Wellington and joined Total Life Changes, a Multi-Level Marketing Company. Chanita was named Rookie of the Year by NTWRKR Magazine, for her ability to earn $250,000 in seven months. Taking the industry by storm, this rookie has spoken on panels and in front of audience, of over 3000 people, sharing that you can become a six-figure earner with any company at any age. Believing in multiple streams of income, her other business ventures include being the owner of the Rock Star Brand, a marketing and event planning company, Urban Christian RockStar Properties, Little Words Big Impact t-shirt line, and Divas and Cowboys.

Walking in purpose, Chanita is a passionate philanthropist. Her passion fueled her to start Beyond The Game, which is a nonprofit that assists the widows and orphans of Swaziland, Africa. Beyond The Game feeds 1000 children 365 days a year. Nicknamed Baby Oprah, Chanita has built a school in Swaziland, Africa, and helped fund many other major projects in that area, including: three Care Points, two Angel Houses, where eighteen orphans live full time, and an Adult Education Center. Chanita has also been able to fund the digging of two wells and pays the school fees for multiple children. Beyond her own nonprofit, she lends her philanthropic hands to many organizations including: traveling to Haiti with Black Celebrity Giving, Autism Speaks, Hip Hop for Cancer, Kandi Cares, 40 Girls and Some Shoes, and B.E.S.T Homes. Each day she dedicates time to changing the world.

As a mompreneur, she recently invested capital for her children to start a business called The Jump Company. Her eleven-year-old daughter is the CEO and speaks on panels often. Chanita is a proud military mom. Her eldest daughter serves in the United States Navy and has been deployed multiple times on the USS Cole. This bragging mom also has two ranking National Champion cheerleading daughters and a young gymnast. Her only son is now married, and Team Foster grew to seven children when adding daughter in law, Della, who is expecting in December 2017. Currently, Chanita is working on a children's cook book with Team Foster.

Her passion for helping people make their dreams come true, has her sharing time residing in Atlanta, Georgia and Johannesburg, South Africa.

**Connect with Chanita Foster on Social Media**

**Website ChanitaFoster.com**
**Facebook www.Facebook.com/ChanitaFoster**
**Twitter @ChanitaFoster**
**Instagram @ChanitaFoster**

**Get Social with my Endeavors**

**BeyondTheGame.org**
**TotalLifeChanges.com/ChanitaFoster**
**LoseAPoundSaveALife.com**

CPSIA information can be obtained
at www.ICGtesting.com
Printed in the USA
FSHW02n1622210518